DR. AL LONG

LEADERSHIP TRIPOD

A NEW MODEL FOR EFFECTIVE LEADERSHIP

Leadership Tripod

Al Long

ISBN 1-929478-42-9

Cross Training Publishing
317 West Second Street
Grand Island, NE 68801
(308) 384-5762

This book is manufactured in the United States of America.

Library of Congress Cataloging in Publication Data in Progress.

Published by Cross Training Publishing,
317 West Second Street
Grand Island, NE 68801

Editor: Bobbie Sease

DEDICATION

This book is dedicated to Vince Myer, a man who cares about those he leads. His life illustrates in teaching and personal example the essence of true Shepherd Leadership.

A PERSONAL NOTE

In my life I have been very blessed to have observed and served under some very effective leaders. While some were Theory X leaders, they were effective in their individual situations and sometimes exhibited aspects of other leadership theories as well.

Vince Myer, the man to whom this book is dedicated, has always been and continues to be a Theory SE leader, something you will learn more about in this book.

I have had the privilege of knowing, observing, and under leadership by Vince for forty-five of my fifty-five years of life. He started out as my baseball coach when I was ten years old. Instead of driving us relentlessly as some coaches do, he shepherded us with compassion and love. I am totally convinced that I would not be where I am today, blessed with the beautiful family I have, had it not been for Vince's selfless example of leadership.

You see, Vince cared about those he led.

Of the many times he intervened on my behalf, one example stands out. Growing up in Advance, Indiana, I was the poor kid from the unpainted house on Wall Street. Believe me, Wall Street in Advance, Indiana during my childhood wasn't anything like the Wall Street of today's evening news. Vince knew my home situation and never treated me as less important or worthy of his attention than any other kid. Others certainly knew how to "rub it in," but not Vince. As a matter of fact, he wanted to be sure I had the same opportunities others had.

You see, Vince cared about those he led.

On one specific evening during my sophomore year in high school, Vince showed how much he cared. I held a job, but happened to take that evening off to play basketball at open gym. Vince was my basketball coach. Taking me aside where no one else could hear us, he asked me if I needed shoes. I ducked my head in embarrassment and shuffled my feet. Then I finally answered yes because, of course, I did need shoes. He proceeded to tell me to go to the local sporting goods store and pick up a pair he had already paid for.

That gesture of kindness is a lesson I've never forgotten. Taking a personal interest in those he coached and reinforcing their sense of self-worth are ways that Vince cared for those he led. Thanks, Vince!

It is my hope that this book will encourage others to be the kind of leader Vince Myer was and continues to be today.

Dr. Al Long

ACKNOWLEDGEMENTS

It goes without saying that no one could create a book on leadership without the help of many people in the process. I would be remiss, however, if I did not take the time to specifically thank some very special people who helped to bring this book to life.

First, I want to thank my wife (of more years than we both want to put down in writing) for all the support and "prodding" to finish strong. She not only encouraged, but also gave wonderful ideas and suggestions on how to strengthen the manuscript's content. Sometimes she was even very direct. On more than one occasion she said, "Just do the job." My love and respect for this lovely lady of God cannot be adequately measured or put into words.

Brian Johnson and Jeff Sickmeier also deserve much credit for expanding the original concept of the leadership tripod. My thanks to Brian for making the tripod three-dimensional and to Jeff for helping to develop the tripod braces.

Finally, thanks to the rest of my family:

Tad, Brad, and Chad for being the fine Theory SE leaders of your families that you are, despite having been Theory X'd through most of your younger years.

Mom, for instilling in me a strong work ethic and aspects of your own goal-oriented personality.

Mary and Joe, for being excellent Shepherd leaders.

Cathy, Kathy, and Dee, for loving me and being Shepherd mothers to my grandchildren.

And Abby, Tyler, Victoria, Trevor, Trey, Deacon, and Baby Blessing–for being the loves of Grandpa's life!

INTRODUCTION

Another book on leadership? That's just what we need, isn't it? Someone telling us everything we're doing wrong, then magically providing the answers to our leadership problems. That's not what this book is all about. Coming from a background that includes extensive leadership experience in the fields of business and education, I know enough to say there are no easy, magical solutions. This book is the culmination of several years of study, observation, and personal experience. It also includes valuable input from colleagues and friends in a variety of occupational settings.

While many books have been written and continue to be written about leadership, few give a real-life application model to judge whether or not effective leadership is taking place in any given situation. *Leadership Tripod* is designed as a practical approach to studying leadership and identifying the characteristics of effective leadership. The leadership tripod concept was developed as a visual model to help organizations evaluate progress toward more effective leadership. The tripod model gives organizations and organizational leaders something substantive to compare to what is actually happening within their organizational culture. Like a surveyor or photographer's tripod, the leadership tripod has legs and braces. These are the leadership elements or principles we will examine in this text. Further, the leadership tripod rests upon a base, just as a functional tripod must be level before it can be used properly.

Within this book the reader will examine not only the conceptual framework of the tripod's individual elements or principles, but will study real-life examples of these principles. The reader will also assess various organizations' successful and unsuccessful attempts to implement the model. Along the way, we will discuss traditional leadership theories, as well as introduce the reader to a new leadership theory.

Each chapter ends with a self-assessment, allowing the reader to evaluate his or her current status and where that individual would prefer to be instead. These assessments are designed not only for the individual's improvement, but also for the betterment of the organization.

In helping the reader better understand what effective leadership is and is not, Leadership Tripod targets:

- Leaders–of corporations, organizations, businesses, etc.
- Those who lead or train leaders, and
- Those under leadership

As you can readily see, this target readership involves almost everyone, for most of us fall into one or more of these categories. At different stages of our lives, we may be both leader and led, trainer and trainee. Most important, we all have room for improvement.

As I sit on the balcony of a beautiful condo in Bonita Springs, Florida, I can't help but relate leadership to the sight before me. The beautiful ocean is like one of the alluring leadership positions I have been offered over the years in business and education. The ocean is powerful and full of possibility, just like many of the leadership positions I have undertaken. But the ocean is also untamed and relentless, continually pounding the shore. Leadership carries with it heavy burdens of responsibility. As leaders, we are like the solid rocks on the shore, attempting–sometimes in vain–to hold back the ocean, trying to protect the shore from the never-ending onslaught of waves, trying to calm the fears and meet the needs of the organizations we lead. Like the rocks on the beach, the harsh reality is that leadership can only withstand the pounding of the surf if it is securely anchored to a firm foundation.

Let us begin our journey in Leadership Tripod by examining the structure of the tripod, seeing how each element contributes to overall effectiveness in leadership. Later, we will look at additional tools to fine-tune the fundamentals. Throughout our study we will evaluate the responsibilities of those who select and support leaders to see what their roles are as well. All of this should contribute to a solid model for studying and evaluating leaders and leadership.

The leadership tripod cannot totally control the ocean, but it can serve as a model to help equip the leader and his or her organization with foundational principles, assuring that the ocean won't wash the sand from under the rocks. It will also help the leader and the organization better withstand the turbulent waters of today's fast-paced, sometimes cutthroat world.

My hope is that after reading Leadership Tripod–whether as a leader, one who is under leadership, or as one who is responsible for the selection and support of leaders–you will better understand what true leadership is and how to effectively apply proven leadership principles to every aspect of your life.

CONTENTS

Dedication   3

A Personal Note   5

Acknowledgements   7

Introduction   9

Pre-Assessment Test   15

1. Leadership: A Look at Leadership Theories   23

2. Solid Support: The Leadership Tripod Legs   43

3. Braced on Focus: Strategic Planning   65

4. Braced on Accord: Communication   85

5. Braced on Principle: Morals/Ethics   103

6. It's Foundational
   Culture: Behavior and Beliefs   113

7. Inside the Leader's Briefcase   123

   Conclusion: Palette of Knowledge   135

   Appendix   141

PRE-ASSESSMENT TEST

Note to the reader: Please take this test before you read further.

In order to measure improvement, one must know where to begin. This pre-assessment instrument is provided to give you a base of reference or knowledge starting point. A post-assessment instrument is included at the end of this book, intended to measure the impact of what you have read. Those of you who are highly competitive or who get anxious when taking any kind of "test," relax.

There are no right or wrong answers. These assessment instruments are designed simply to give you an idea of your knowledge base regarding the topic of leadership–before and after reading Leadership Tripod.

1. In your organization, what is the level of knowledge in leadership theory and application for each of the following groups?

Those selecting leaders:

5	4	3	2	1
High	Moderate	Neutral	Some	None

The leaders themselves:

5	4	3	2	1
High	Moderate	Neutral	Some	None

Those under leadership:

5	4	3	2	1
High	Moderate	Neutral	Some	None

2. Are each group's job and/or leadership responsibilities clearly stated?

Those selecting leaders:

5	4	3	2	1
High	Moderate	Neutral	Some	None

The leaders themselves:

5	4	3	2	1
High	Moderate	Neutral	Some	None

Those under leadership:

5	4	3	2	1
High	Moderate	Neutral	Some	None

3. Does each group have authority to clearly carry out its responsibilities?

Those selecting leaders:

5	4	3	2	1
High	Moderate	Neutral	Some	None

The leaders themselves:

5	4	3	2	1
High	Moderate	Neutral	Some	None

Those under leadership:

5	4	3	2	1
High	Moderate	Neutral	Some	None

4. Are accountability systems clearly established for each group?

Those selecting leaders:

5	4	3	2	1
High	Moderate	Neutral	Some	None

The leaders themselves:

5	4	3	2	1
High	Moderate	Neutral	Some	None

Those under leadership:

5	4	3	2	1
High	Moderate	Neutral	Some	None

5. Is there a strategic plan in place for each group and is it clearly understood and used as a base of reference for all decisions?

Those selecting leaders:

5	4	3	2	1
High	Moderate	Neutral	Some	None

The leaders themselves:

5	4	3	2	1
High	Moderate	Neutral	Some	None

Those under leadership:

5	4	3	2	1
High	Moderate	Neutral	Some	None

6. How would you rate the communication lines within each group (intra-communication)?

Those selecting leaders:

5	4	3	2	1
High	Moderate	Neutral	Some	None

The leaders themselves:

5	4	3	2	1
High	Moderate	Neutral	Some	None

Those under leadership:

5	4	3	2	1
High	Moderate	Neutral	Some	None

7. How would you rate the communication lines between each group (inter-communication)?

Those selecting leaders:

5	4	3	2	1
High	Moderate	Neutral	Some	None

The leaders themselves:

5	4	3	2	1
High	Moderate	Neutral	Some	None

Those under leadership:

5	4	3	2	1
High	Moderate	Neutral	Some	None

8. Are the organization's ethics and morals clearly stated and evident?

Those selecting leaders:

5	4	3	2	1
High	Moderate	Neutral	Some	None

The leaders themselves

5	4	3	2	1
High	Moderate	Neutral	Some	None

Those under leadership:

5	4	3	2	1
High	Moderate	Neutral	Some	None

9. Is the culture (climate) of the organization healthy and do the behaviors and beliefs of each group match that culture?

Those selecting leaders:

5	4	3	2	1
High	Moderate	Neutral	Some	None

The leaders themselves:

5	4	3	2	1
High	Moderate	Neutral	Some	None

Those under leadership:

5	4	3	2	1
High	Moderate	Neutral	Some	None

10. How important do you think the concept of leadership is to each of the groups below?

Those selecting leaders:

5	4	3	2	1
High	Moderate	Neutral	Some	None

The leaders themselves:

5	4	3	2	1
High	Moderate	Neutral	Some	None

Those under leadership:

5	4	3	2	1
High	Moderate	Neutral	Some	None

11. What do you hope to get from reading Leadership Tripod?

CHAPTER ONE

LEADERSHIP: A LOOK AT LEADERSHIP THEORIES

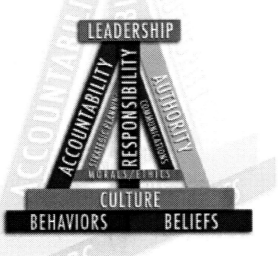

A Look at Leadership Theories

Countless books and studies have focused on leadership, especially in recent decades. The fact that leadership is essential for personal and organizational growth is undisputed. *How* leadership is best cultivated and facilitated, however, is the subject of much debate. This chapter will briefly survey various leadership theories, identifying key concepts and seeing how they relate to the top piece of our leadership tripod.

Trait Leadership Theory

One of the earliest leadership theories, originating in the early part of the twentieth century, Trait Leadership Theory assumed that by studying certain very effective leaders specific leadership traits could be identified and categorized. Leadership traits were first studied in a military context. However, it didn't take long for those hiring leaders in the nonmilitary sector to adapt the essential principles to their context, trying to predict success by matching a specific leadership trait to a leadership candidate.

The Right Fit

In looking at how Trait Leadership Theory might apply today, let's take someone who is being considered for a leadership role in a weight loss company. If this person overeats and is obviously overweight, he or she probably will not be the best "fit" for the position—metaphorically speaking. Further, if this leadership candidate does not truly believe in the importance of healthy eating habits and physical fitness, he or she will undoubtedly have a tough time leading the organization and "selling" the idea that weight loss is important. Thus, those reviewing candidates for this position would be looking for the *trait* of discipline in a candidate's personal life.

Profiling Key Traits

Just recently a university was looking for a new dean for its graduate school of business and education. In the initial meeting of the leadership team, members were asked what they would look for as they reviewed candidates for the position of dean. Team members immediately began to profile the ideal candidate, listing characteristics they saw as important to this leadership role. Among several things mentioned were that the dean should be open, cooperative, and experienced. The members of this college leadership team were actually beginning to identify *traits* they felt were essential in order for the dean to successfully lead the college.

At first glance the "modern" student of leadership theory might quickly dismiss the Leadership Trait Theory as too simplistic and even passé. However, trait leadership theory has continuing value even in contemporary society. The problem is in relying *only* on traits in selecting a leader. The leadership candidate for the weight loss clinic might possess the trait of personal discipline, but still have poor managerial skills. The college dean might be open and cooperative, but be unable to prioritize his appointments. Although traits play an important role, leadership is more than the sum of traits.

Behavior Leadership Theory

Looking beyond traits as the primary criteria for identifying leaders, the Behavior Leadership Theory instead decided to focus on the behaviors of effective leaders. This theory essentially involved comprehensively analyzing the behaviors of effective leaders, identifying which behaviors are most responsible for success in leading others. Candidates matching those patterns of behavior were seen as the most likely to fill a leadership position successfully. The behavior leadership theory also lent itself readily to organizational adaptation; i.e., properly interpreted, certain behaviors could be taught to leadership trainees.

Which Behavior is "Right"?

In looking again at the weight loss clinic, the human resources director might look for a leader whose behaviors coincide with the mission or current needs of the company. Such behaviors might include not only physical fitness and a daily workout regimen, but also dedication to the company and a history of staying with a company for an extended period of time. If the weight loss clinic were experiencing financial difficulties or personnel problems, they might target someone able to "clean up" the company. Thus, they would want a leader with a proven history—someone whose past behaviors included the ability to streamline the workforce by fostering cross-training and eliminating unproductive or superfluous employees.

Similarly, the college searching for a new dean might look for behaviors such as team development and the ability to

delegate responsibility to his or her directors. The leadership
committee might also want the dean to lead by modeling the
behaviors they felt were important. These could range from
actually teaching classes and meeting regularly with all facul-
ty and staff to expecting the dean to belong to a certain
denomination, attend athletic events, and join service clubs.

Qualifying Effectiveness

The Behavior Leadership Theory is also problematic and
somewhat simplistic. Even though it can be used as a guide to
help profile what the decision-makers are looking for in a
leader, this theory cannot guarantee that identifying certain
behaviors will necessarily produce a good leader. No leadership position can be studied in totality, assuring that all
behaviors are categorized and then taught and/or learned.

The weight loss clinic could hire a leader based on behavior criteria and still not get out of the red. The new college
dean could demonstrate all the applicable behaviors and fail
at helping the college meet its mission. Conversely, the dean
could demonstrate none or very few of the desired behaviors
and still be a very effective leader.

Traits and behaviors are important building blocks in con-
structing an ideal leadership candidate, but they do not com-
prise the entire person.

Situational Leadership Theory

The Situational Leadership Theory as developed by
Hersey and Blanchard is based on the premise that a person
can be an effective leader if placed in the proper situation.[1] An

extrapolation of this theory would suggest that a person who is highly ineffective in one situation of leadership might be highly effective in another.

Short-Term or Short-Sighted?

Given the two scenarios we have been using, let us first examine the weight loss clinic. The situational theorist would say that even though our overweight leadership candidate might not be a "fit" for the clinic, he or she might make an excellent leader for a crisis intervention center, where weight is not the key issue. Situational theory also points to circumstance as affecting outcome. For example, a leader might seem to achieve great success by increasing membership and bringing the clinic into the black. However, if there has been a recent upswing in the area's population—most notably, an increase in the number of health-conscious residents—the leader more likely may have benefited from favorable circumstances rather than leadership expertise.

Situational leadership is evident today when corporations in trouble bring in a leader to "turn the company around". Decision-makers and corporate boards allow this kind of shake-up because of the difficult situation in which they find themselves. There's a sense that the new leader will be effective because he or she will only be there for a short time.

The error in this thinking is precisely its short-term focus. Effective leadership isn't measured by someone's ability to swoop in and make dramatic changes that temporarily affect the bottom line. That line on the chart may rise sharply, but most likely, it will descend again just as quickly. Short-term decisions often have long-term effects that are not examined through the lens of situational leadership theory. For example, perhaps the new leader advocates ridding the company of computer-illiterate employees and hiring only those with computer savvy. As a result of the "shake-up," did the company lose some valuable and loyal people? Do the new computer-literate employees lack depth and experience? Might the company have avoided this collateral damage by offering its employees computer training instead?

McGregor's Theories

In studying how leaders lead, Douglas McGregor categorized them into two camps: Theory X and Theory Y.[2]

Theory X Leadership

According to McGregor, the Theory X leader basically believes that those he or she is leading inherently want to do the very *least* expected of them. The Theory X leader believes all employees need to be watched carefully and driven hard, or the work won't get done. If left on their own, the "workers" will take from the organization, doing as little work as possible and getting away with as much as they can. Theory X leaders have people working *for* them rather than *with* them. The term micromanager is usually associated with a Theory X leader.

An organization and those responsible for selecting leaders can be Theory X in nature as well. In this kind of organization, the leader is required to show "heads rolling" in order to prove "effective" leadership. Unfortunately, when problems come, the organization and the leadership will look for people to blame instead of problems to solve.

Defining Success

Ironically, many Theory X organizations are viewed as highly successful. I held a leadership position not long ago in an organization that believes in Theory X leadership. When going through the selection process, it was apparent to me that the organization had long believed in Theory Xing its staff and leaders. This was totally contrary to my style, but the organization's board adamantly professed a desire to change the way they had been managing. They wanted a leader with a very different style, one capable of taking them from where they had been and leading them in a new direction. They sincerely seemed committed to this change, even though their peers in the corporate world viewed them as highly successful just the way they were.

The problem came when I actually started trying to go in a new direction. The board had been used to micromanaging for so long that when I didn't follow that style, they couldn't adapt to the change. They felt that if they were not privy to all decisions and if people weren't constantly being targeted for dismissal then progress was not taking place. They *talked* about change, but it was soon evident to me that they were not comfortable with change.

As a leader with a different leadership style, I might have quickly jumped to the conclusion that I was right and they were wrong. However, the fact remains that this organization was capable of meeting its goals without a change in leadership style. It goes back to the original discussion of Situational Leadership Theory. In this particular situation, as I learned firsthand, Theory X leadership was probably adequate for this particular organization.

Theory Y Leadership

McGregor's second theory is called Theory Y. As might be expected, this is the antithesis of Theory X. Theory Y leaders believe that those they work *with* inherently want to do the very best they can for themselves and their companies. Left to themselves, the associates will work hard and share a sense of accomplishment when their company succeeds. Theory Y leaders believe their job is to do everything they can to assure that those who work with them have all the tools and resources they need to be successful. If the workers are not successful, Theory Y leaders will first look at themselves to see if they have failed to provide the environment necessary for achievement. Rather than blame people for underachievement, they examine the system or the root problem. Whereas the Theory X leader faults *people* for failure, the Theory Y leader faults the *process.*

Steady as She Goes

Those who know me would probably tag me as a Theory Y leader. I recently led an organization which could also be characterized as a Theory Y organization. It took eight years for this organization to make the transition from Theory X to Theory Y. The difference with this organization is that the board which hired me had carefully planned a logical transition to a Theory Y mentality. Everyone was committed to the change, so the change was implemented successfully–even though it didn't happen overnight.

Theory Z Leadership

William G. Ouchi originated a leadership style labeled Theory Z.[3] Its similarity to McGregor's Theory Y lies in Ouchi's belief that people do want to achieve success both for themselves and for their companies. How this success occurs and the roles of the leaders in helping people achieve success is what differentiates Theory Z from Theory Y.

Whereas McGregor would say that the leaders should make the success of the workers their primary task, Ouchi suggests that the leader should create an environment in which teams work together for the success of all. Leaders would be responsible for fostering joint decision-making and cross-functional teams. The atmosphere would be one of cooperation and shared decision-making, as well as shared accountability. Rather than having the leader decide what needed to be in place in order for the workers and the organization to achieve success, it would be up to all stakeholders to jointly analyze and decide the best direction and structure so all could achieve maximum success.

Applying Theory Z

Organizing teams and allowing these teams to decide the direction of the organization may not work in every situation. But many manufacturing firms are finding the Theory Z leadership model as extremely viable. Where previously many such companies were organized in a highly mechanistic, bureaucratic manner, the ever-changing nature of manufacturing today frequently necessitates quick decisions at the basic floor level if firms are to remain competitive. This involves decentralized decision making; i.e., bypassing the cumbersome "chain of command" that can slow or paralyze production. Many Japanese companies, especially in the technology sector, follow this organic model, readily lending themselves to Theory Z leaders and leadership.

Sorting It Out

What then should a leader do when faced with a leadership position that does not coincide with his or her leadership style? There really are not many good alternatives. To avoid this kind of situation, leaders and those selecting leaders need to do a thorough job of prescreening candidates for compatible styles. Still, even a thorough prescreening cannot guarantee the ideal candidate for the organization or prevent unforeseen circumstances from changing the original criteria. Faced with such a mismatch, there are only two options: 1) the organization can make the appropriate changes to adjust itself to the leader's style, or 2) the leader can find a different position. Both of these options can be stressful to all involved, but not nearly as stressful as conflicting ideologies about how to effectively lead an organization.

Theory S Leadership

I propose still another theory: Theory S. The S stands for Shepherd. As I have studied leadership over the years, I've looked for the ideal model to embody the finest in leadership principles. The shepherd seems to best exemplify that ideal model. I envision two subdivisions to my shepherd model. SW leadership represents a Western culture shepherd. SE leadership represents an Eastern culture shepherd.

Fostering a Relationship: The Eastern Shepherd

My wife and I had the unique opportunity to visit Israel, where modern-day culture rubs elbows with ancient ways and traditions. While visiting a tell in Samaria, we saw a shepherd tending his flock much as shepherds have done for hundreds of years. There was a sense of tranquility in the scene before us. Even more, it seemed that the shepherd and his flock were comfortable together and that the sheep completely trusted him. We learned that in the Eastern culture a shepherd creates a summer sheepfold each evening and leads his flock into its protection for the night. As the sheep pass individually through a small opening, the shepherd puts his staff or rod across the opening. He does this to check each animal for injuries and overall stamina since they have been in open pasture all day. After seeing to their needs, applying medicinal ointments if necessary, and determining that they are safe, he then lies down across the small opening–effectively presenting himself as a barrier to any predators or thieves that might try to enter the sheepfold.

Driving the Flock: The Western Shepherd

Shepherds of the Western culture tend their flocks very differently from what we observed in Israel. The Western shepherd "drives" the flock, generally using a dog to nip at the sheep and herd them where the shepherd wants them to go. The shepherd/sheep relationship is different, too. When the shepherd yells at the sheep, they move–not because they want to, but because they fear him or her. There is no long-term relationship between the sheep and shepherd. In fact, it's a one-way relationship, all for the benefit of the shepherd. In Western culture, sheep are a commodity and are essentially raised for wool and meat. That's a win-lose situation–the shepherd wins and the sheep ultimately lose.

Theory SW Leadership

How does all this relate to leadership? Let's look at the owner of a restaurant. The food is good and the place is always busy. The owner and his family are well known in the community and thought to be one of the wealthiest families in the county, maybe even in the state. So why am I choosing this organization as an example of Theory SW Leadership?

The reason is the way he treats his employees. The community is full of disgruntled past employees. You see, this leader believes the workers are there only to serve his needs. If they fail to do that or if they make any kind of mistake, they are out! He leads by intimidation; the "dogs" that nip at the heels of his employees are his managers, usually other family members who share in the profits of the business. Further, this leader pays minimum wage, uses the most downtrodden to his benefit, and then callously discards them. His philosophy is that there is always someone in need of a job, so he gets what he can from his workers, then replaces them like tissue paper.

This "shepherd" doesn't care to know his sheep and his sheep definitely don't know him. If they knew beforehand what they were in for, they probably would never agree to work for him in the first place.

Theory SE Leadership

Let's replace the current owner of the successful restaurant with a Theory SE Leader, one who leads the way an Eastern shepherd would lead. An Eastern Culture Leader (SE) would care individually about his or her workers and attempt to run the business in a way that would benefit all. He or she believes in the workers and feels an obligation to make their lives better. This is not to say the SE leader or owner abhors financial success! Not at all. But the driving force or motivation for making the business profitable is to include the workers in the success. The relationship between owner and workers is long term, leading to mutual celebrations of longevity. There is no need to "drive" the employees to do their work. Instead, the SE leader examines different ways to ensure employee happiness and success. Many times I have found these SE leaders to have a heartfelt desire for their employees to share in the profits of the company.

The SE Leader should not mistakenly be labeled as a business wimp or one who is careless about making money. What I have found in my cursory study is just the opposite. These leaders many times are self-made men and women who know business well and know equally well how to succeed. What they do not have in common with the SW Leader is the idea that workers are just another commodity. They share with other SE Leaders a belief that a successful business is successful *because of* the workers, not *in spite of* them.

It's Not Just a Job

Recently I did a strategic planning seminar for a Theory

SE leader. I didn't know this was his style of leadership until he told me what he hoped to gain from the seminar. His goal obviously wasn't the "bottom line," because he shut down his business and made the necessary arrangements for all his employees to attend. He simply wanted to learn about strategic planning *with* his employees so they could all achieve success and feel a sense of "ownership" in the success of the business.

I can just hear some of you who are reading this right now! "You've got to be kidding," you might exclaim. "No business owner would even *think* that way, much less make it happen!" Well, if that is what you are thinking, you probably are operating from a Theory SW mind-set. Unlike some other business owners I've known, this owner sincerely wanted to help the company grow and increase its profit margin so those working for him (*with* him, he would say) could reap some of the benefits.

I don't want to leave the impression that he didn't want to make money in the process; he just wanted to make sure that all involved in the company's success benefited from that success. His belief was and continues to be this: if employees can see a chance to share in the growth and success of the company, they will work to ensure the company's success. In the process, they enjoy their work and don't regard it as "just a job."

As evidence of the owner's sincerity in arranging for the seminar, by the end of the day the owner and employees had adopted a specific objective–the creation of a profit-sharing plan to be implemented within the first six months of the upcoming year.

It was also interesting during the day to observe the close-knit relationship these individuals shared with one another. Not that they were alike in many ways, but it was evident that they cared about one another—not just at work, but outside work as well. There was talk about hockey, soccer, vacations, kids, and ailing family members. It was obvious that the employees knew the owner and the owner knew his employees.

Investing in the Future

In *The Seven Habits of Highly Effective People,* author Stephen Covey talks about making *deposits* into an emotional bank account.[4] I saw that demonstrated throughout the day of the strategic planning seminar. The owner had an *investment* in his employees beyond monetary parameters. He was also open to his fellow workers in a personal, vulnerable way, allowing them to know him as a caring human being. The *deposits* he made that day, and continues to make in his routine business practices, are something from which he can withdraw in tough times.

An Egalitarian Ideal

Sergeant Mike Strank was one of the men who died raising the American flag at Iwo Jima. He wasn't a corporate executive or a business owner. He probably didn't know anything about strategic plans, mission statements, or leadership models. But he was what his men called a "Marine's Marine," the best leader they ever had. This must have been true because they followed him into that firestorm at Iwo Jima. Here's how one of them described Mike shortly before they landed:

-        Mike is their shepherd. He has won their con-
        fidence . . . Mike, the immigrant American, is
        representative of the best of the young leaders
        in the Pacific. A sergeant, he does not lord his
        rank over anyone. He embodies the Raider
        egalitarian ideal of no divisions between the
        men, no hierarchy.

        He eats with his men instead of going to
        the sergeants' mess. And a few weeks before
        leaving for Iwo Jima, Captain Dave Severance
        tries to recommend Mike for the rank of Pla-
        toon Sergeant. Mike turns the offer down on
        the spot, saying, "I promised my boys I'd be
        there for them."[5]

Mike was the embodiment of the SE leader. He led his
men; he didn't drive them. He knew and cared about them,
ultimately giving his life with and for those he led. Those he
led followed him into battle—many of them to their own
deaths—because they trusted him. That's what SE leadership
is all about.

Summary: Know Thyself

As you have seen in this brief survey, there are admirable
qualities in each of the leadership theories. However, it is a
huge mistake to exercise the principles of one theory alone—
especially those who are seeking to become an effective leader. Sticking with one leadership theory leaves an important
component out of the equation—those you are leading.

The truth is that effective leaders find themselves using

aspects of all the theories at some time during the challenging business of leading. It is important, however, to do a careful self-analysis to determine your dominant leadership methodology. You must know how you *tend* to lead before you can ever do anything to improve your leadership style.

You must also have an understanding of how those you are trying to lead need to be led. For example, let's say you are a Theory SE leader. You believe in your employees and want them to succeed so the company can succeed. However, one of your employees consistently arrives late for work and doesn't fulfill the requirements of the job you have given him. Because of this, he is adversely affecting the morale of the other employees and the business as a whole. You care about him, but feel he is taking advantage of you. What do you do? Quite simply, if you really care for the employee, you may have to Theory X him for a while in order to best serve his long-term interests. My experience has been that the most effective leaders are those who understand various theories, applying the appropriate principles at the appropriate times–ensuring the success of the company and the employees.

Self-Assessment Exercise:

1. Write down which leadership theory you believe is your normal style. List five specific examples to demonstrate how you operate from this theory.

2. When you are under leadership, what circumstances make you feel most productive and fulfilled?

3. When you are under leadership, what circumstances

make you feel most negative about your tasks?

4. How do you think others would view your ability to lead?

5. Do you need to alter your leadership style? If so, why? How do you propose changing? If you do not feel the need to alter your leadership style, why do you believe you are successful in your present style?

Finally: Share the results of your self-assessment with someone you know will be truthful with you. Have him or her assess your answers and see if you have an accurate picture of your leadership characteristics. Many times, how we perceive ourselves and how those we are leading perceive us are two very different things. It is important to know ourselves *and* those we lead.

[1] For example, see Paul Hersey and Kenneth H. Blanchard, *Management of Organizational Behavior: Utilizing Human Resources,* 4th ed. (Ontario: Prentice-Hall, 1982).

[2] For more information on McGregor's theories, see Douglas McGregor, *The Human Side of Enterprise* (New York: McGraw-Hill, 1960) and *Leadership and Motivation* (MA: MIT Press, 1966).

[3] For more information, see William G. Ouchi, *Theory Z* (Avon, NY: Avon Books, 1982).

[4] Stephen Covey, *The 7 Habits of Highly Effective People: Powerful Lessons in Personal Change* (New York: A Fireside Book, 1990).

[5] James Bradley and Ron Powers, *Flags of Our Fathers* (New York: Bantam Books, 2000), 132.

CHAPTER **TWO**

SOLID SUPPORT: THE
LEADERSHIP TRIPOD LEGS

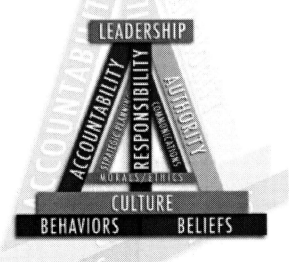

The Leadership Tripod Legs

In our leadership tripod model, the top piece would be meaningless without something upon which to stand. The tripod itself provides that support, making possible true, effective leadership.

A few years ago when I first began to construct this model in my mind, I came up with the idea of a triangle. The three pivotal elements–responsibility, authority, and accountability–certainly fit that triangle model. Each is dependent on the other. If one is absent, the model is flawed. Thus, leadership cannot and will not be effective.

The triangle is one dimensional, however. I was looking for a model with more depth, one that would convey the idea of structural support. The tripod was the perfect solution. The image of three legs supporting the primary concept captured the essence of what I was trying to depict–providing a stable base upon which leadership could anchor itself. If a leg were missing, the tripod could not stand. If a leg were weak, the tripod could collapse. If the legs were not of equal length, the top piece would be in danger of falling. A leader could have all the skills, traits, and behaviors necessary for success, but without the three supporting legs of responsibility, authority, and accountability, he or she would not be able to effectively lead an organization.

Ask yourself these questions:

1. Can a leader lead effectively if he or she is given *responsibility* and held *accountable*, but is not given the *authority* to make decisions?

2. Can a leader lead effectively if he or she is given *responsibility* and *authority*, but then is not held *accountable?*

3. Can a leader lead effectively if he or she is given *authority* and held *accountable*, but is given no *responsibility?*

In my opinion and as the result of years of both leading and observing leaders, I believe the answer to be an emphatic *no* to all the questions above. Each of the three legs is equally important in assuring that leadership is securely held in place. If they are not structurally sound and firmly planted, effective leadership will be compromised—and the organization and those being led will not reach their full potential for excellence.

As we take a look at each of these three legs, I ask you to relate what you learn in the next few pages to your own organizations and to your own experience as a leader or potential leader. I think you will find, as I have, that this tripod model is applicable to any situation you can think of.

Responsibility

The word *responsibility* probably means many things to many people. Therein lies the fundamental reason why the responsibilities of a leader need to be as clearly defined as possible. Those in leadership positions realize all too well how difficult it is to put down on paper the responsibilities entailed in their everyday schedule. It isn't as simple as just listing them and then checking them off as you accomplish them each day! Some things seem to defy description. For example, a leader is expected to facilitate intra- and interdepartmental communication, develop networking with other organizations, establish rapport with personnel and clients, and a host of other hard-to-define responsibilities. Not exactly the same as checking items off your weekend chore list, is it?

The Importance of a Job Description

When it comes to itemizing job responsibilities, most of us immediately think of that familiar term: the *job description.* Familiar or not, it is amazing to me how many large companies, school corporations, small businesses, and churches lack even the most basic job description for *any* level of responsibility–leader or those under leadership. Most often, the tasks are simply done and no one knows specifically what is entailed in positions outside one's own sphere of responsibility, nor how these various areas relate to one another. While an organization can function this way for a while, problems arise when a gap occurs: someone leaves, is injured or falls ill, or even dies. Organizations with no clear-cut job descriptions then scramble to fill the void. Many times tasks are not completed, clients are left hanging, and money is lost because no one initially took the time to list the specific responsibilities for the position in which the void occurred.

Avoid a Power Play

A dangerous situation can sometimes occur in organizations that allow people to develop the responsibilities of their own positions–without requiring them to document these responsibilities. Such people can cling tightly to their positions without ever allowing anyone else to know the specifics of their jobs. This is called wielding "expert power," a kind of power play most frequently seen in long-time employees who want to insure job security. "If no one else knows what exactly it is that I do," such a person reasons, "no one else can take my job." For obvious reasons, a leader cannot allow this to happen in any organization he or she is expected to lead. I have personally seen this kind of power play cripple organizations, essentially rendering them helpless because of an unexpected void in a key position. For example, what would happen if the only person who knew the combination to the bank vault died overnight of a heart attack?

All Dressed Up and No Place to Go!

The opposite can also occur if detailed responsibilities are not given to leaders and those they are supposed to lead. A leader or an employee cannot be expected to perform effectively if each is not given a job description.

As hard as it is to believe, this does happen all too frequently today. It even happened to me. Not long after I retired from an organization, I was asked by that same organization to take a higher leadership position than the one I had held previously. I told the friend who offered me the position that I would take it on an interim basis until he found someone permanent. After all, I was looking forward to retirement!

So I rearranged my life to fit the time requirements of the position and decided to tackle the task with enthusiasm.

Much to my surprise and dismay, I found I had no new responsibility above and beyond what I had done before. I essentially had been promoted, but found myself doing nothing more challenging than my previous duties. Because I was not given the responsibilities associated with the position, others picked them up. Many times people who take on these additional responsibilities in the leader's absence think doing so will strengthen their positions in the company or organization.

This is not a good situation for any organization and can be very demoralizing for a new leader. When a new leader is selected for a position in which responsibility has been shifted to others, or others have taken the responsibility upon themselves, it may be difficult for the new leader to recapture the responsibility he or she needs to be an effective leader. Anyone confronting such a situation needs to immediately "reclaim territory" or he/she will be ineffectual.

Off Center

Without the solid leg of *Responsibility*, the Leadership Tripod cannot stand. It will be off-center and in danger of crashing to the ground–taking with it the hopes and unrealized potential of those affected in any way by leadership.

What is the answer, then? For maximum efficiency and overall stability, leaders, those who locate and place leaders, and those under leadership need job descriptions and job responsibilities to be as specific as possible. If they are going to be given authority and held accountable for the functions of their positions, it only makes sense for them to know the specifics of their responsibilities.

From Custodian to CEO

In creating job descriptions for an organization, no position is exempt, whether custodian or CEO. While some
employees may "look down" on the custodial aspects of their
organization–pointing to the lower pay scale and perceived
lower status of custodians–I know for a fact how instrumental this position is to the smooth operation of any organization. My father was a custodian in a school setting. Let's compare the everyday responsibilities of a school custodian as
they relate to the education of the children. Then, let's look
at the everyday responsibilities of a school board member or
even the superintendent. If the school board member and the
custodian were to fail in their respective responsibilities for
one day, which do you think would most impact the students
that day? Which abdication of duty would most negatively
affect the learning environment, preventing students from
learning and teachers from teaching? Which one–the custodian or the school board member–could be absent for a day
and probably not even be missed? This gives one pause for
thought, doesn't it?

The job description for a school custodian is certainly
more than a one-page "clean your area" kind of summary. It
involves everything from coordinating the cleaning and maintenance of facilities, to the types of chemicals to be used and
their proper application, to the correct storage of those chemicals and disposal of waste, to the proper care and maintenance of equipment–and doing all of this in keeping with the
school's mission statement: assuring each student a quality
educational experience because of the custodian's part in
preparing, maintaining, and cleaning the rooms in which that
education will take place.

Securing the Strong Leg

All areas of responsibility in an organization should have job descriptions with that kind of detail, laying out specific tasks and timeline expectations. Many firms will make a cursory attempt at the more high-profile positions, but seem hesitant to take the time to profile job descriptions for every position in an organization. One very efficient way to accomplish this seemingly daunting task is to ask the employees themselves to help in the creation of the job descriptions. This will give employees a part in implementing organizational policy, at the same time demonstrating how the company values them and their place in the organization. The initial work of creating job descriptions will be well worth the effort, resulting in more competent cross training and promotions, as well as timely and efficient replacement decisions.

To be as effective as possible and to continue to improve their competitive edge, organizations must develop *Responsibility*, placing its strong leg securely under their leadership team.

Authority

Webster's Dictionary defines authority as (n) *"the right and power to command and be obeyed or to do something."*

I think we capture more of the grit of this word when we look at the verb form of the definition: (v*)* *"to give legal power or right to."*

In leadership, the power and right to make decisions is the authority a leader needs to carry out leadership effectively. A leader can be given much responsibility, but if not then given the authority to fulfill the responsibility, his or her leadership will be undermined.

Running on Empty

Let's compare a leader to the owner of a fine car. He has been equipped with an adequate means of transportation and even may have been given a road map to guide him to his destination. But someone forgot to put gas in the tank. After traveling a short distance, the gas tank runs dry and the driver is forced to pull the car over to the side of the road.

Given responsibility (and maybe even a detailed job description) but no fuel (authority), the leader is left behind, unable to move forward or merge with traffic, unable to travel down the road of self-improvement and company success.

Why does this happen? Why would any organization give a leader or prospective leader responsibility but not the authority to fulfill the obligations (and potential) of that responsibility? I have come to the conclusion that some of those who hire and place leaders are either frustrated individuals who would like to be leaders themselves, or are power hungry and insecure, exercising control over a situation by "controlling" the leader. It is counterproductive in every way, but it is a phenomenon I've seen over and over again.

Foul Ball!

We are all familiar with major league baseball club owners famous for "dis-empowering" their managers. Although they select and hire their leaders–which is their prerogative as principal owners–they all too often undercut their leaders' ability to do the job they were hired to do. News stories abound of continual intrusions, overstepping the authority of the managers, making decisions the manager should make, and keeping the team in constant turmoil. As a result, some club owners have gone through an embarrassingly long list of managers and general managers over the years. This is a classic example of how to effectively sabotage responsibility: shut it down by refusing to activate it with the corresponding catalyst of authority.

In *The 21 Irrefutable Laws of Leadership,* John Maxwell states, "Only secure leaders are able to give power to others."[1] I believe that to be true not only of leaders, but of those who select leaders. If a board, owner, supervisor, team leader, or any other person or group cannot release power to the leaders under them, allowing these leaders to make and implement decisions, the organization, company, leadership group, team, or even family will fall short of its full potential. In fact, withholding authority can lead to disaster.

Learning the Hard Way

President John F. Kennedy is one of our most admired and beloved presidents. But even he had to learn a lesson about leadership the hard way. In making the decision to invade the Bay of Pigs, he played it close to the vest. History tells us that he held tight reins on those in authority, made the major decisions himself, and listened to few people outside the close-knit inner circle of his Cabinet. In doing this, a kind of "Group Think" took place. Many advisers who should have been involved in such an important determination were left out of the decision-making loop. Even though their offices and roles carried appropriate responsibility, they were given no authority to make suggestions or decisions. If President Kennedy had allowed them to exercise their authority, the decision most likely would have been *not* to invade. But we did invade, with disastrous results.

However, in another situation, President Kennedy did make the most of his leaders and advisers, allowing them to exercise their authority and seriously weighing their recommendations. He also included proven leaders outside the Washington circuit, empowering them to speak their minds and allowing them to make decisions. In so doing, he defused the volatile Cuban Missile Crisis–one of his greatest achievements and finest hours. President Kennedy relinquished power and trusted his leaders to do their jobs–not necessarily giving him what he wanted, but what they thought to be the best possible solution to the problem.

Two critical situations handled in two totally different ways with dramatically different results.

I am told that Theodore Roosevelt once said, "The best executive is the one who has sense enough to pick good men to do what he wants done, and self-restraint enough to keep from meddling with them while they do it."

This statement pretty well sums up what leadership authority should be. Those who refuse to share authority believe they are making themselves and their organizations stronger. In fact, the opposite is true.

Hoarding Authority

The devastating effect of hoarding authority is well illustrated in the failure of many small businesses to make it to "the next level." In this scenario, an entrepreneur starts a business and is the primary force behind its growth and success. Then the business arrives at the point where it outgrows the entrepreneur's ability to lead it by him or herself. The leader faces an important decision. Does he or she hire managers and give them the responsibility and authority to expand the growth potential, or does he or she continue to "run the show" all alone? Unfortunately, if the owner hoards authority and responsibility, he or she will experience one or more of the following: 1) the owner/entrepreneur will burn out, 2) the company will remain at status quo, or 3) the company will begin the slow slide to failure. If the original founder of the company does not carefully select and mentor a successor, there is a high probability that the company will not continue to exist after the original founder is out of the picture. Hoarding authority will most assuredly choke the life out of the very dream he or she had for the company's success.

On the Other Hand

Just as denying authority to those in leadership positions can debilitate an organization's forward movement, so too can granting too much authority. Granting authority without sufficient checks and balances (accountability) can be destructive to effective leadership and can sabotage the entire organization. As we saw earlier in our discussion of responsibility, a leader or one under leadership who is given absolute authority without the corresponding balance of accountability is in danger of wielding expert power.

To reiterate, expert power exists when someone in the organization has knowledge that no one else in the organization has. If that person is terminated, leaves voluntarily, or becomes incapacitated, the organization can suffer a crushing blow because of the void that person leaves.

I know of a small corporation with a technology leader who had expert power. He was the only one in the organization with the passwords to enable the computer system. When he suddenly became critically ill, the corporation was literally incapacitated because they couldn't access their computers. Valuable time and resources were lost until they located an outside "expert" to override the system.

The technology leader of this organization had been given responsibility and authority. However, no one had held him accountable for seeing that an emergency plan was in place to prevent just such an organizational collapse. With that in mind, let's turn to the third leg of the leadership tripod—the leg of accountability.

Accountability

Not long ago on my way to the university, I was reminded of what *accountability* means in a very personal (and expensive) way. Driving with my sunroof open, I was really enjoying the cool rush of air around me, the early morning sunshine, and the smell of newly mowed grass. You know how a car just seems to run smoother after it has been washed and waxed? Well, if you do, you can picture the joy I was experiencing as my freshly cleaned car cut swiftly through the cool morning air on my drive through beautiful central Indiana. Swiftly is the operative word here. I was having such a good time, I failed to realize I was speeding. Just as I thought things couldn't get any better than this, I spotted a distinctive car in the opposite lane–a beautiful black car with many antennas and the markings of the Indiana State Police. Instinctively, I checked my speedometer and realized I was going at least ten to twelve miles per hour over the posted speed limit. Glancing guiltily in my rearview mirror, I saw him nimbly turn around and head my way. No doubt about it: I was about to be held *accountable* for my decision to drive over the speed limit. This lesson in accountability cost me $99.50! That amount would make most of us say, "Ouch!" But just think how much more expensive the cost was for the company that didn't hold its technology expert accountable for his actions?

Is Accountability a Negative?

In successful leadership, accountability is not an option–it is a necessity. This third leg of the tripod is essential for leaders, those who choose leaders, and those under leadership. Without it the organization will never be what it should or could be.

But why is accountability necessary? We have only to look at our government's fundamental structure to see the reason why. Our founding fathers created the executive, legislative, and judicial branches of government as a check-and-balance system; i.e., to keep one leg of government from overpowering or dis-empowering another. The leadership tripod works in the same way. Accountability is necessary as a check and balance to assure that all tasks are completed, to assess the organization's movement toward continuous improvement, and to determine if employee and organizational needs are being met. If performed properly, accountability will help all the personnel as well as the organization reach their highest potential.

Over the years, the main problem I have seen in the judicious use of accountability is in how it is *perceived*. Many who select and place leaders, leaders themselves, and those under leadership see accountability in a very negative light. They see it as a punitive method rather than as a tool meant to foster their growth and effectiveness, as well as that of the company or organization. In this "negative" light, accountability has been seen primarily as a performance evaluation, telling people what they are doing wrong. In a more "positive" light, however, it can be used to affirm their worth and motivate them to improve.

"Likert" or Not

Many companies and most organizations employ a standard procedure to *evaluate* the staff. This term even suggests a "summative" process of sorts to determine if a person stays or goes. The Likert Scale is one such evaluation method, listing categories on a scale of one to five–one representing "strongly disagree" and five representing "strongly agree." Sometimes the scale is reversed and sometimes more than five numbers are used. But in those narrowly defined and impersonal categories, a person's value is measured. The evaluation may attempt to broach the areas of goal setting or self-improvement, but generally this process is highly subjective and evaluator-driven, with little if any input from the one being evaluated.

Future-oriented leaders must replace the negative "keep-or-lose-your-job" focus of the evaluation form and develop a positive paradigm of improvement through accountability.

Formative, Not Just Summative

To be effective for all those involved in an organization, my belief is that accountability must be "formative" as well as "summative." What I mean by formative is that accountability should not just be judgmental, based on what the person has or has not done. Accountability should also be a mutual attempt to identify and describe what the person needs to do to improve, what specific things can make him or her a better employee or leader. By making this a mutual effort, employees are not only held accountable for what their supervisors say they must do, but they learn valuable, transferable skills designed to improve them and make them well-rounded individuals. This gives them "buy-in" on improvement at all levels. This improvement process should also be tied in to the overall improvement (strategic plan) of the organization. In this way, the person understands and internalizes how through his or her individual improvement the organization can move toward the corporate goals it has set for all concerned.

I have been working with two different organizations recently to totally redesign their methods of accountability. What has traditionally taken place for many years in these organizations is this:

Job description---Some sort of documentation----Evaluation

What we are trying to create now is far different and will take time to fully implement into the organizational culture:

Job description---Assessment--------Verification

Instead of using Likert Scales, we are developing rubrics to assess the achievement of success and the level of success attained. This will take most of the subjectivity from the assessment process, thus reducing the level of apprehension in both the assessor and the one being assessed. The huge difference between the two methods is that the person to be assessed or held accountable will know *beforehand* how he or she will be assessed and what specifically he or she will need to achieve. The one assessing, as well as the one who will be assessed will know up front what both are looking for and what has to take place for successful achievement of the goals.

This process will be viewed not as a method of *separating*, but of *improving*. The leader will not be looking to "catch the person doing something wrong" (Theory X, SW), but rather will be looking at how they can both work together to improve themselves and the organization as a whole (Theory Y, Z, SE).

Exceptions

Just as we saw earlier in the section on responsibility, there will still be instances when a very specific, documented "do-it-or-you-won't-stay-here" type of evaluation will be necessary. There are always those who simply won't do what they are supposed to do, no matter how you try to motivate them. Unfortunately, accountability necessitates removing them from their jobs for the good of the other employees and the organization as a whole. This is certainly not pleasant, especially in the traditional evaluation process. But the damaging effects can be minimized by a change in the assessment process, one based on formative values. Prior to dismissal, those involved will have been made aware of potential problems well in advance and will have been given ample opportunities to make needed improvements.

Summary: Driving Home a Point

All three legs of the leadership tripod–*Responsibility, Authority,* and *Accountability*–must be present for effective leadership to occur. Those under leadership must also be able to identify and understand these principles. To "drive home" my point, let's look at my experience with the state trooper as it relates to this model.

The State Trooper

It was evident the state trooper knew his *Responsibility.* He understood his job description because it was very specifically laid out for him in the code of law by which our state operates. He knew what he was supposed to do. He knew on that lovely spring morning that his specific assignment was to cover State Highway 37 in Madison County. He also knew he had the *Authority* to stop a certain motorist for going too fast and to issue him a ticket. He knew further that if he didn't do his job correctly he would have to face *Accountability* in a court of law. Therefore, he filled out the ticket correctly and made sure the motorist knew why he was issuing the ticket.

What would happen, instead, if the trooper:

- had responsibility and was held accountable, but had no authority to issue the ticket?
- had authority and was held accountable, but was given no responsibility?
- had responsibility and authority, but was not held accountable?

I believe you can use your imagination to envision the chaos that could take place.

The Driver

What about the driver? He had *Responsibility* because he had read the driver's manual, knew the laws, and knew the posted speed limit. He had *Authority* because he could make the decision on how fast to drive, where to drive, what to drive, etc. He also certainly was held *Accountable* for his actions when the officer pulled him over and issued him a ticket.

What would have happened, instead, if . . .

You can take yourself through the same exercise above and get the picture. The ramifications of a driver not being held accountable for speeding could result in the ultimate price: the loss of his life or the life of someone else.

Self-Assessment Exercise

1. In your leadership position, are your responsibilities clearly defined?
    a. If yes, how?
    b. If no, why not, and what can you do to change this?

2. Do you as a leader make clear the responsibilities of those you lead:
    a. If yes, how?
    b. If no, why not, and what can you do to correct this?

3. In your leadership position, do you have the authority need to do your job effectively?
    a. If yes, how?
    b. If no, why not, and what can you do to change this?

4. Do you as a leader give those you lead the authority they need to do their jobs effectively?
    a. If yes, how?
    b. If no, why not, and what should you do to correct this?

5. In your leadership position, are you held accountable for your actions and performance?
    a. If yes, how?
    b. If no, why not, and what can you do to change this?

6. Are those you lead accountable for their performance and improvement?
    a. If yes, how?
    b. If no, why not, and how can you change this?

[1] John Maxwell, *The 21 Irrefutable Laws of Leadership* (Nashville: Thomas Nelson, 1998), 124.

CHAPTER THREE

BRACED ON FOCUS: STRATEGIC PLANNING

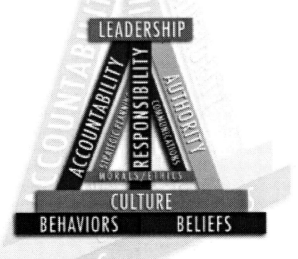

Strategic Planning

Introduction: The Tripod Braces

I would like the reader to visualize the Leadership Tripod and imagine a huge boulder suddenly dropped onto the top piece or platform of the tripod. Supporting this enormous weight are the three solid legs of Responsibility, Authority, and Accountability. Although they manage to hold up under this burden for a while, eventually the unrelenting weight is going to take its toll. The stress on the legs will be too much and they will weaken, tilt, or collapse under the pressure.

I thought about this in the early stages of developing the tripod model. The legs themselves were not enough to ensure structural viability. But braces would strengthen the tripod, giving additional support to the legs and helping to distribute the weight.

This, of course, is a perfect analogy for our study of leadership. What components are necessary to strengthen and improve a company through its leadership? In my years of consulting with a variety of companies and organizations, I have identified three characteristics or "constants" essential to bracing the leadership tripod, pulling it together and making it strong:

1. An effective strategic planning process and plan implementation.
2. Effective and ongoing analysis of communications.
3. Values and beliefs upon which a company builds strong ethics and morals.

In this and the next two chapters, I will discuss these three characteristics in detail and give specific ways to implement them. Those in leadership positions can sometimes be overwhelmed by the enormity of their tasks and the sheer number of people for whom they are responsible. Like the boulder sitting on the tripod platform, without a solid framework to bear the burden of leadership, the whole structure is in danger of collapse.

Fate or Focus?

We hear a lot about strategic planning these days. It's one of our most popular "buzz" phrases. So why is it significant, and why have I chosen *strategic planning* as one of the braces holding the Leadership Tripod together?

In my own eight-year experience of moving a company from a Theory X to a Theory Y frame of reference, I have found strategic planning to be indispensable in developing the company's course and fostering overall improvement. I have also read and studied extensively and consulted with flourishing companies, "picking the brains" of successful leaders. All of this has reinforced my belief that strategic planning is instrumental in making leadership effective and in moving a company toward continuous improvement.

Strategic plans are not just for big corporations and organizations. Individuals and families can benefit greatly from strategic planning. About ten years ago, I created a strategic plan for my own life. It has been one of the most significant events in my life and in the life of my family. The process caused me to look more deeply into how I was living, compelling me to prioritize my actions and create a self-improvement plan.

A company without a strategic plan is like a ship without a rudder. It most certainly can move across the water, but no one knows where it will end up. Likewise, an individual or family without a plan embarks on a journey through life with no road map. Where they end up is wherever fate takes them, and that most likely is *not* where they can live most fully and productively.

Over the past several years, I have taught strategic planning principles and have had the opportunity to facilitate the strategic planning process in many areas and situations across the country. The different types and sizes of the companies do dictate somewhat the time necessary to develop an effective plan, but the process works in companies of any size or setting—just as it will work well with individuals and families. It is a simple, but useful way to plan for continuous improvement.

Thinking Strategically

My first question to a group trying to learn about strategic planning is this: "If you don't know where you are going, how do you know when you get there?"

The simplicity of this question underscores a truth few individuals and companies take seriously. Many families, companies, churches, and even organizations operate in a totally *reactive* mode, almost never exercising control over their destiny by taking the time to plan strategically.

My family and I recently made an emergency trip to Cincinnati to be with my brother who had just suffered a heart attack. When we were given the message, did we just jump in the car and take off? No, we called and got the name of the hospital, then searched the Internet for specific directions on how to get there.

Had we just jumped in the car and sped away, we might somehow have found the hospital, but it would not have been without great loss of time, many frustrations, and possible dangers. By taking the time to plan strategically and set out our goals, we were able to make efficient use of our time and we arrived at the hospital safely, serving our family's needs in a most effective manner.

Why should we do anything less for our families or for the organizations we serve?

Streamlining the Process

Another observation I have made over the past few years is the time and effort many companies waste trying to develop a strategic plan. While recognizing the need for a strategic plan, they have been thwarted in their efforts because they have been sold a process that is cumbersome and time consuming. I know of one corporation that spent thousands of dollars and eighteen months in developing a plan that still has not been completed. The stakeholders became frustrated with the whole ordeal. For eighteen months everyone had been talking about change and direction, but nothing had happened. If you can't develop a plan in a much shorter time frame than eighteen months, then you are probably not using a method conducive to productive planning strategies.

The simple process I have developed has been field tested and proven to be effective. Of course, it continues to improve–that's the point of strategic planning, after all. Many of the earlier idiosyncrasies were a natural outcome of trial and error, but all were useful in helping to sharpen and streamline the process and make it more user friendly.

Establishing Parameters

Some preparatory work is necessary before launching into the work of building a strategic plan. The company or organization will need to decide who is going to be involved in the planning group, how often to meet before and after the plan is established, who will be responsible for "activating" the plan, and how to assure that everyone is on the same page when it comes to interpreting the purpose of the plan.

Get Them Involved!

The makeup of the planning group is critical. What I have found over the years is that the more stakeholders are included in the process, the more effective the planning and strategic plan will be. Initially, until the decision-makers understand the process, they may need to create a rudimentary plan or prototype for the overall company. As soon as possible, however, as many levels of stakeholders as possible should be included in the process and allowed to modify and fine-tune the prototype. This will give them a sense of ownership in formulating the plan, rather than feeling that those "in charge" imposed it on them.

Visit It Often

The planning process isn't over when the strategic plan is

created. A strategic plan isn't a document that is filed away and forgotten. Strategic planning is ongoing. At the very least, the planning process should take place annually. Some companies in fast-changing competitive environments may have to plan on a more frequent basis. Once the plan has been completed, it should be revisited on no less than a quarterly basis. If possible, organizations and companies should revisit it even more frequently. In this way, the company expresses to its constituents the importance and viability of the strategic plan.

Activate It

The plan also needs to include details on its activation. How will it be implemented, and who in the organization will be responsible for making sure each phase is completed? Some leaders mistakenly believe that once the plan has been completed, their responsibility is to oversee and complete all the items contained in the plan. Rather than make the leader stronger, this just adds more weight to the "boulder of responsibility" pressing down on the leader, something that will only weaken that person.

In *Leadership by the Book,* the authors write, "Leaders often just don't know how to develop people, and they end up doing all the work themselves. In addition to burning themselves out, their people remain dependent on them and underdeveloped."[1] This is what could and sometimes does happen if leaders don't share the responsibility of putting the plan into action.

Understand It

Some leaders don't understand that the strategic plan is a guide, not a barrier to continuous improvement and change. As I mentioned earlier, the process I will be discussing has been modified through trial and error. One corporation I led through the process seemed to flourish. It appeared the plan was being implemented very effectively. I called the leader to see how things were progressing. He said enthusiastically, "Great! Every time someone comes in to ask to do something, I just pull out the plan. And I say, 'So, if it's not on the plan, we won't be doing it.'"

Obviously, this leader had to be mentored further! He had to learn that the goal of a strategic plan is not to *limit* what a company can do; it should just set the minimum level of progress for improvement. Now each time I lead an organization through this process for the first time, I try to impress upon them that planning is a minimum standard of success, not a maximum.

The Strategic Plan: A Model

If the reader can imagine a body of water with no banks, you can imagine a company, family or organization without a strategic plan. There may be many good things in the water, but without boundaries and direction, the water becomes essentially a swamp. We equate swamps with stagnation; very little of anything positive come from them.

If, however, you put banks around that same water and give the water direction, it begins to move. Flowing water is active and more productive. It can generate electricity, give wildlife nourishment, become a habitat for fish and other animals, provide people opportunities for recreation, etc. So it is with companies, families, and organizations. They can be much more productive if given the direction of a strategic plan.

The appendix of this book contains an example of a corporate strategic plan, as well as a personal strategic plan. These plans are from a *real* company and a *real* person. After you have read the specific sections of the Strategic Planning Model below, go to the appendix and read the corresponding elements in the real-life examples.

The Strategic Planning Model below flows in a circular direction. As those who have studied or completed a strategic plan realize, a circle never ends. To be effective, a strategic planning process must be ongoing–constantly being updated to assure that the individual or organization is on track for continuous improvement. The following model is understandable and easy to apply:

Strategic Planning Model

Let's examine the individual components of the model to see how you or your organization can readily adapt this model to your particular circumstances.

Vision: How Do You Want to Be Remembered?

As the model shows, the first action in a strategic planning process should be the creation of a *vision statement.* In his discussion of vision statements in *The Seven Habits of Highly Effective People,* author Stephen Covey suggests thinking of how you or your organization *wants to be remembered.* In this light, the vision statement should be long term and should address what the company or individual ultimately wants to become. A company should think five to ten years out, asking itself: If we could design the "perfect" situation ten years from now, what would this company look like?

Each company or individual may have different ideas about what a vision statement should contain. As well, the vision statement should custom fit the individual or company. But certain elements are common to all vision statements:

1. It should be relatively brief and written in future tense.
2. It should be based on an analysis of the company's current status and goals.
3. It should be believed and disseminated from the top of the organization.
4. It should set the long-term direction of the entire company.

What a Vision Statement is Not

The description above seems succinct, uncomplicated, and to the point, doesn't it? However, you would be surprised at how many *vision* statements are really *mission* statements.

The key difference is that a mission statement contains no long-term thinking. Many of the vision statements I've read do include some of the elements above, but they are so lengthy and cumbersome that leaders, those placing leaders, and those under leadership cannot "connect" with the vision. If those who are supposed to be striving toward a vision cannot embrace it, the vision will lack credibility.

It is also readily evident that many so-called vision statements are simply catch phrases or clusters of motivational sayings meant to inspire those already toiling on a daily basis to toil even harder—without clearly addressing the purpose of the toil.

Analysis is Key

Neither of these interpretations captures the essence of an effective vision statement. To customize a vision statement to the particular concerns of an individual or organization, it must be based on a thorough analysis of the company's infrastructure. Leadership books abound with analysis techniques. Three of the best analysis techniques I've found in my experience are:

1. SWOT – an acronym derived from analyzing a company's **S**trengths, **W**eaknesses, **O**pportunities, and **t**hreats
2. Beliefs Audit – analyzing a company's core values
3. Stakeholder Analysis – identifying any person or group who will be affected in any way by the organization.

These three kinds of analyses, as well as others, make the planners think about whom they serve, what they believe, and what they need to do to become the very best they can be. In writing your vision statement, before you can plan where you ultimately want to go, you need to analyze where you have been and where you are at present. It is extremely important for the primary leader to be involved in this vision-setting process, because if the leader doesn't totally agree and buy into the vision, the strategic plan will not succeed.

Start Your Engines!

As I write this chapter of the book, it is May in Indiana. Naturally, many Hoosiers are excitedly anticipating the Indianapolis 500. Let's imagine a young driver just coming up the ranks of open-wheel racing. He or she is serious about making a career of racing. With this in mind, let's help this driver establish a strategic plan for the 2003 calendar year.

VISION: *I will become the next great Indianapolis 500 race driver and be remembered as one of the best race drivers of all time.*

With the vision in place, the next step in the process is to establish the mission statement.

Mission: Focusing on Present Tense

Just what exactly is a *mission statement?* It is what an individual, organization, or company is about *today.* It answers the question, "On a daily basis, what do I (or what does the organization/company) actually do?" Like the vision state-ment, the mission statement should be fairly short in length, easy to remember, and easy to embrace. All too often, how-ever, I've seen mission statements that are paragraphs long and cumbersome. Full of well-intentioned statements, they miss the mark of what a true mission statement should express: the ongoing, daily mission of the company. The mis-sion should flow logically into the vision. The pivotal thought is this: "If I fulfill my mission, I will ultimately get to my vision."

Keep It Specific

Much of the work entailed in establishing a vision state-ment can be adapted to the mission statement. This includes the analysis of the company's purpose and objectives. How-ever, the mission's focus is of shorter term and should be more specific. It reflects the process from vision to objectives; i.e., going from very general to very specific principles. The mission should also be reevaluated each time the strategic planning process takes place, whether semiannually or yearly.

While the vision statement is expressed in future-oriented language, the mission statement should be in present tense. It should reflect where the company, individual, or organization is today, not where it wants to be.

Let's look at our race driver's mission and see if it meets the criteria above.

MISSION: *I am an open-wheel racer who is practicing, competing, and learning about my sport each day, continu-ing to improve my skills as a racing driver on my way to participating in the Indianapolis 500.*

The questions we must now ask are these: If this driver continues to fulfill his/her mission, can he/she ultimately fulfill the vision? Does this mission statement logically flow into the vision? If it does, then it is an acceptable mission statement.

Goals: Aiming for Success

After the company has established its mission, it needs to direct its attention to setting *goals*. When facilitating this process with companies, I encourage them to avoid being overly aggressive the first time through in determining goals. Establishing three to five goals during the first planning session is sufficient to activate the mission and move it toward achieving the vision. The goals should flow logically from the mission and be in line with the analyses completed earlier during the vision planning session. Goals should be based on the corporation or individual's areas of need or emphasis. Achieving the goals will enable the organization or individual to continuously improve, fulfill the mission, and move toward the vision. Many times when helping a company establish goals, I use the results of the beliefs audit to custom fit the goals to the company's mission. Basing goals upon core beliefs is not only a natural progression but is also quite logical and pragmatic.

Let's return to our Indy driver. During the beliefs audit, he/she made this statement, "I believe that to be a 500 champion, you must 'pay your dues' coming up." We can assume the driver has been "paying dues" for some time and is ready to take the next step toward the vision. If that is the case, we can phrase a goal as follows:

GOAL: *I believe I can pass my rookie test in 2003.*

As you have probably already surmised, the next question is this: If the driver fulfills this goal, will that help to fulfill the mission which, in turn, will ultimately help to achieve the vision?

If so, the goal is acceptable. If not, the goal should be revised to make sure it *does* flow logically. If the goal is acceptable, the next step is to create objectives to help reach the goal.

Objectives: Measuring Success

Objectives are the real meat of the plan. They are the action items that when evaluated help to determine progress. Establishing objectives involves setting guidelines or rules, just as with the vision, mission, and goal-setting sessions of strategic planning. When I facilitate this process with companies and organizations, I try to form a template that can be used through the entire process.

In building objectives, I look at two aspects. First, I generally preface each objective with something like this: "I (we) will . . . (action to take place)." Second, I establish a timeline, clearly indicating how long the objective will take to complete.

These two parts, the action and the timeline, give a concrete way to evaluate whether or not the objective has been met. That is the single most important aspect of the objective. It *must* be measurable. We do not just say an objective has or has not been completed. We ask, "What are the specific measurements of success?"

Just as I encourage companies to avoid being overly aggressive in establishing goals, I also encourage them to be a bit conservative in establishing objectives. Usually three to five objectives for each goal are plenty to handle the first time through.

In looking at our driver's goal for 2003, let's set some specific, measurable objectives for him/her to achieve in order to attain that goal . . . which will help to fulfill the mission . . . which will help to achieve the vision.

OBJECTIVES:

1. By June 1, 2002, I will obtain a full-time ride for the remainder of 2002.[2]
2. I will qualify and participate in four IRL races before May 1, 2003.
3. I will test at Indy in October 2002.

Now, of course, come the inevitable questions: Are the objectives specific and measurable? Will accomplishing these objectives help the driver achieve the goal, which will help to fulfill the mission, which will ultimately help to achieve the vision? If the answers are yes, the objectives are acceptable.

Summary: Standardize the Vision

The first of the tripod braces is the strategic planning brace. This chapter's discussion has underlined the importance of strategic planning in helping to strengthen the Leadership Tripod. Without a plan, leadership flounders. With a plan, leadership has direction and focus. For organizations, companies, families, or a leader's personal life, the significance of effective planning cannot be overstated.

If suborganizations within a larger organization create their own strategic plans, these plans need to flow logically into the larger organization's strategic plan. Each goal and objective should meld with and assist in achieving the corporate vision. In fact, when facilitating the strategic planning process, I always urge subgroups to keep the same vision as the larger group.

Maintain Perspective

After having facilitated and carried out many strategic plans and processes, I have one final suggestion for those wishing to begin this process. Do *not* use an in-house person to facilitate the strategic planning process. Someone outside the company or organization will have a much more objective approach, will see the company through an unbiased lens, and will have the impartiality necessary to give a fair and candid appraisal. However, it is important for the facilitator to be knowledgeable about strategic planning, thus avoiding overextension of the process. As I mentioned earlier in this chapter, taking too long and spending too much will hinder rather than improve the company's chances of establishing a viable strategic plan. Remember, a good facilitator also has a mission. And he or she will skillfully pursue that mission to create an environment conducive to the strategic planning process and to aggressively expedite the process—for the good of all involved.

Self-Assessment Exercise

1. Do I know my company's vision and mission statements? Does what I do on a daily basis help to fulfill the vision and mission? If not, why not? (If your company has vision and mission statements, write them below.)

2. If you have a vision for your own life, write it below. If you don't have one, begin the creation process by writing down some thoughts for your vision.

3. If you have a mission statement for your life, write it below. If you don't have one, begin the creation process by writing down some thoughts for your mission.

4. List at least three of your company's goals, or list three goals for yourself or your family.

5. List at least two measurable objectives for each of the goals.

6. Read the strategic plans in the appendix of this book. Did they meet your expectations of what a strategic plan would look like? What did you learn from reading these two plans?

[1] Ken Blanchard, Bill Hybels, and Phil Hodges, *Leadership by the Book: Tools to Transform Your Workplace* (New York: William Morrow and Co., 1999), 55.

[2] A full-time ride means a driver is part of a fully funded IRL (Indy Racing League) team for a complete season of racing.

CHAPTER **FOUR**

BRACED ON ACCORD: COMMUNICATION

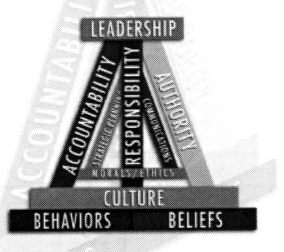

Communication

Although the strategic plan helps to stabilize the tripod, one brace is not enough to ensure structural stability. As can be seen in the diagram above, we still need two more braces to make the tripod as strong as it can be. This chapter will focus on the second brace, *Communication*.

The Big "C"

What I have found over the years is that people complain a lot either about communication in general or the lack of effective communication in an organization/company/family. However, few do anything *but* complain. During this discussion of communication, I will not only try to give general principles of effective communication, but also to give specifics on how to improve and evaluate the communication in an organization. My premise is straightforward: *Unless those placing leaders, the leaders themselves, and those under leadership can communicate effectively, leadership will not be as strong as it should be in order for the organization to achieve at its highest level.*

A couple of years ago I referred to "The Big 'C'" in one of my articles.[1] I wasn't talking about Cancer, but Communication instead. The focus of my article was the misconception of communication. It is my opinion that most of those who complain about a lack of communication view it to be a *one-way* passing of information from the top down to those under leadership, or from the leader on up to those who place leaders. If either end of the spectrum believes this to be the case, "communication" will always be an exercise in frustration.

That is why everyone in an organization needs to have a better handle on what communication actually is and what their roles involve in making sure effective communication takes place.

Misconceptions

Of course, to say that effective communication is important in creating a healthy corporation, family, or organization is to state the obvious. However, I still don't see much real analysis of communication problems or specific solutions designed to enhance and improve communication for both internal and external customers.

I also see far too many top-level executives clinging tightly to the "one-way" interpretation of communication, while those under leadership have a completely different perception. I recently asked a vice president of an organization how he would rate his organization's lines of communication. His answer spoke volumes. He answered, "Oh, they're great! We send communications to all our staff all the time." His perception was that if he sent out information on a regular basis, and if it was received and acknowledged, he was thus "communicating."

Most of his staff didn't share that same perception. They told me that although they were being sent "stuff," no one was really communicating with them.

The same is true viewed from the other side. Many leaders feel the very ones they are trying to lead don't communicate with them. They may assert that they believe in an "open door" policy, but wonder why no one feels free to come through the "open door."

These common misconceptions about communication require specific kinds of intervention in order to create a shared perception.

Defining Communication

Essentially, communication is the passing of information between at least two parties. This can take many forms, as I will attempt to explain in this chapter. In my experience, communication only becomes effective when both parties understand what the communication was designed to do.

To say it another way, for communication to take place, someone must create it (encode it) and then someone must receive it (decode it). Between the time it is encoded and the time it is decoded many things can and often do happen. Some authors refer to an interruption in the flow of the communication as "noise."

The Effect of Noise

Of course, this "noise" can take many forms. It actually can be noise as we know it. For example, those attending a NASCAR race would have trouble communicating verbally during the race.

Noise can also refer to the emotions of the encoder or decoder. Let's say that a leader is trying to communicate an important message to someone under his or her leadership—*at the same time* the person under leadership has just learned of a family tragedy.

I'm familiar with this kind of noise. I was teaching an MBA class, the last class the students had to pass before they graduated. I had explained the requirements and time lines to the students. Late in the course a student told me she wouldn't be able to complete her final assignment. I was a little irritated (to say the least) because it was evident she hadn't "heard" what I had encoded to her about the requirements for the course. I proceeded to "tell" her again that she would indeed complete the assignment and I would accept no excuses. After a few times of trying to break through the "noise" of my emotions, she finally managed to encode her message in a way that I could decode it. Her son had been convicted of felony murder two days earlier. Once we both cleared the air of emotional noise, we were able to decode what the other was saying and come to a solution to the problem.

I was recently watching a TV commercial for cell phones. The actor in the ad made a very profound statement: "Isn't communication great when it works?" Many times, noise can damage communication or even render it worthless. The actor was referring to actual noise in the transmission of the message through the cell phone. Sometimes what one person says is not always what the other person hears. Such is the case in the commercial. For true communication to take place, the receiver has to be able to decode the message the way the encoder wanted it to be understood.

The Missing Link

While very basic, the model below demonstrates the key principles for effective communication. In order to be sure a message has been decoded correctly, there needs to be some link back to the one who originally encoded the message.

Without that link, how does one know the communication has been received and understood the way it was intended?

Methods

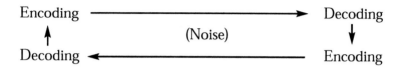

To repeat, I see too many leaders and those under leadership just *assuming* communication has taken place and then getting upset when they find it hasn't. They need to take the time to create a process that will systematically check to see if communication has been successful. This process will save those encoding and those decoding much frustration.

One entity encoding information without a corresponding entity decoding the information is NOT communication. But, sadly, this is exactly what happens in many companies, organizations, and even families.

How We Communicate

Let us take a closer look at specific methods of communication, as well as some of the problems that can inhibit the decoding of information.

Verbal Communication

The majority of the time, whether in our family life or business/organizational life, we communicate verbally. It's a direct and effective method of getting messages across. You might think that very little noise would get in the way of a face-to-face communication between the encoder and the decoder. That is true for the most part, but problems can still occur. Those selecting leaders, leaders themselves, and those under leadership need to understand what these problems are and how to address them. In the area of verbal communication, the two primary problems are the use of the vernacular and the effect of inflection.

Vernacular: It's Greek to Me!

Many times the words we use in the workplace do not translate well to others outside the workplace. This happens when we use acronyms, abbreviations, or "legalese" that those outside our business cannot understand. Therefore, while we may encode in a manner that we understand, the listener may not be able to decode what we are saying. People with limited computer knowledge have only to talk to an authentic computer "geek" to know what I mean.

Just the other day, I was making a presentation to a national health care facility group. We were talking about making decisions and how to implement a logical decision-making process. When I asked them to give me a problem to use as an example, they came up with "Plan B Patients" and their effect on the company. They all knew exactly what *they* were talking about, but I didn't have a clue.

In this kind of situation, a listener many times is too embarrassed to admit that he or she doesn't understand what is being communicated. The listener may also simply decide in his or her own mind what is meant. Both cases are disastrous to effective communication. In my situation, I asked everyone to back up and explain what "Plan B Patients" were and why these patients were problematic to the company. Once we all came to the same understanding (communication had taken place), we were able to get on with solving the problem in a logical manner.

Inflection: Say That Again?

How one says something many times is just as important as *what* is said. The encoder and the decoder may be saying and hearing two very different messages simply because of the way the words are verbalized. An obvious form of this problem occurs when the media edits recorded interviews to attain just the right number of sound bites for the evening news. By carefully (and sometimes unscrupulously) editing the recorded words, technology can make someone sound as if he or she is encoding one message when in fact the speaker may have meant the message to be decoded in an entirely different manner.

Of course, inflection is also an excellent tool in effective communication. By varying or modulating the pitch and volume of one's spoken words, a person can make a lasting impression on an audience. Inflection can vitalize words when presented with emotion or mute them if muttered tonelessly. The same words spoken with different inflections can say very different things to the hearer. Since we don't have a way to give auditory examples, let's preface a simple sentence with an explanation and then, through punctuation, see if we can communicate the significance of inflection.

Preface: You are a supervisor in a manufacturing setting and you need to communicate verbally to someone under your supervision that cleanliness is a concern in the work area. The message you want to convey is that the area needs to be cleaned: "You need to clean up around here." How simple can that be? Surely anyone can understand that, right?

- **"YOU** need to clean up around here!!!!"
  Spoken in a loud voice, the emphasis is on the word *you*. The hearer will decode the message to mean that he or she needs to do the cleaning.
- "You need to clean up around **HERE.**"
  The decoder will probably interpret this to mean that he or she is to clean the specific location of their conversation.
- "You **NEED** to clean up around here."
  The decoder may feel that someone is putting pressure on the supervisor to see that the area is cleaned.
- "You need to **CLEAN UP** around here."
  Is the supervisor referring to the decoder's personal hygiene, telling him or her to have cleaner personal habits while at the workplace?

Hopefully, this example demonstrates how inflection can change the message the decoder is hearing. The supervisor needs to be sure that what he or she is trying to convey is what the employee is hearing, so that the employees understands the verbal message the way it was intended.

The Telephone: A Unique Hybrid

Somewhere between verbal and nonverbal communication, the telephone is also a powerful, versatile, and necessary means of communication. With the addition of the cell phone, every leader is at the disposal of anyone who happens to have his or her cell phone number. While this allows you to stay in touch with the office at all times, it also means you are unable to totally get *away* from the office. When a leader carries a cell phone, the office is wherever he or she might be when the phone rings.

Voice Mail: Even if you can't answer the phone right away, most people now have voice mail. This greatly enhances communication, but comes with problems as well. When used properly voice mail can be a great asset and time saver. When used improperly, it can be frustrating and time consuming. My new catch phrase is "voice mail illiterate." What I have found is that many people just don't know how to use voice mail. For example, let's say you leave this voice mail message: "This is Greg, call me." What if the person you were calling doesn't recognize your voice? What if that person knows ten men named Greg with ten different phone numbers? If your original intention was to talk business, just think what might be going on in that person's mind? Is he or she irritated? Will he or she take the time to go through that list of ten names? What will he or she think of the way you are representing your business? Leaders need to be sure they understand how to leave a message that not only conveys professionalism, but also puts their companies/organizations in a professional light.

Who Answers the Phone? An often-overlooked aspect of a company or organization's "face" to the world is how it han-

dles its phone communication. Is your company's receptionist responsible for answering the phone or does the company
use an automated answering service? When someone calls
your company, does the receptionist make a favorable
impression on the caller? Does he or she convey professionalism and courtesy? If your company uses an automated service, is it user-friendly, or is the caller impersonally shuffled
from one extension to another, forced to listen to a veritable
litany of options? Both verbally and nonverbally, the telephone can either improve or sabotage effective communication.

Written Communication

The idea of a handwritten note or letter seems almost
archaic in today's technology-based society! The phrase
"snail mail" seems to sum up this generation's emphasis on
rapid communication and immediate feedback. But handwritten notes and letters are still very valuable forms of communication. Other "traditional" forms of written communication include memos, directives, and business letters. More
contemporary forms of written communication include E-
mail and fax messages.

Handwritten Messages: The Personal Touch

The Note: Whether you are a leader, one who selects leaders, or one under leadership, the handwritten note of encouragement and affirmation is a powerful tool. It demonstrates
that you have a genuine interest in the one receiving the note
(Theory SE). This is especially meaningful in light of today's

hectic pace and many demands on your time. To take the time to write a note of encouragement speaks volumes to the one for whom the note is intended.

Problem: As one experienced in writing personal notes, I admit that the primary problem with this form of communication is one of expectation. Others will expect this of you. The additional burden placed upon the note-writer can outweigh the positive results of the notes themselves.

Let's say you're a leader in a company. You've noticed that a certain employee has spent extra non-paid time to complete a project. You handwrite a personal note thanking this person for his or her dedication in completing an important task. However, another employee, one you haven't noticed, has spent just as many or even more hours on the same task. But you don't write this person a note. The inadvertent communication this person receives is that his or her work must not be as valuable as the other employee's work. Even though the leader never intended to communicate this kind of message at all, that is what the second worker decoded because he or she did not receive a handwritten note.

The Letter: The personal letter is another nearly lost form of written communication. I personally believe letters–handwritten or typed–to be an important communication that many leaders fail to utilize, especially in sales and marketing. The follow-up letter can be a very significant part of the sales process. By this I do NOT mean a "canned" set of follow-up letters! I know some leaders who think that once an appointment has been completed, all they have to do is hit a key on their computers. They consider the "canned" letter that the printer spews out to be sufficient in thanking a client or potential client for the time spent at the appointment. As one who has received these kinds of letter, I can personally attest that they are NOT effective. A personally written letter and one kicked out of a database are worlds apart. I am especially impressed when I receive a letter that mentions specific things we talked about in our meeting. Such letters don't have to be handwritten, but when they are, the impact is even more significant. A personal letter can add tons into the emotional bank account of leaders, those selecting leaders, and those under leadership–especially in times of grief, celebration, weddings, graduations, and other special occasions in the lives of the letter recipients.

Problem: As with handwritten notes, the sheer volume of letters a person would have to compose could be overwhelming. However, even canned letters can be personalized. If nothing else, jot a quick P.S. on the bottom of the letter. This at least lets the decoder know that the encoder was personally involved with the letter; he or she didn't just ask an assistant to mail a "canned" response.

Electronic Mail: First it was the fax machine, an electronic convenience that is still a major component of the technology revolution. For many in today's electronic age, E-mail has become the communication of choice. It is easy, quick, and efficient. E-mail saves time and resources. No envelopes to lick, no stamps to purchase. It is faster, less cumbersome, and more private than the fax machine. Those needing to meet pressing deadlines can even send documents as E-mail attachments. Feedback is almost immediate.

Problem: E-mail's assets are also its greatest problems. Wow, that sounds like double talk, doesn't it? It's easy, it's quick, it's efficient . . . or is it? Typing a quick E-mail and sending it off into cyberspace seems to rid the encoder of respon-

sibility for making sure the communication has been received
and decoded the way it was intended. This has happened to
me. On occasion I've asked people why they didn't communicate with me as we had agreed. The response? "I sent you
an E-mail. Didn't you get it?" Having met their obligation to
communicate, they felt it was then up to me, the receiver, to
notify them if the E-mail didn't get through.

A second problem with E-mail is that it is impersonal.
Many use E-mail as a shield to keep from having to confront
someone verbally, either face-to-face or by phone. It seems to
be much easier to complain, attack, or belittle by E-mail than
it is to meet someone personally and talk over the situation.

Nonverbal Communication

People have written books on nonverbal communication
alone! How we convey messages through body language,
gestures, facial expressions, behaviors, our sense of personal
space–even what we drive, how we dress, and whom we
hang out with–is a field ripe for analysis and debate. Obviously, I cannot even scratch the surface, except to underscore
the importance of nonverbal communication in our everyday
interactions. Many times it is the most overlooked and yet
most obvious factor in determining miscommunication.

Let me use a recent NASCAR race as an example. The
points leader for the championship needed to make a pit stop.
Another veteran driver was following him. The first driver
motioned with his left hand his intentions and proceeded to
pull to the bottom of the track. He thought he had encoded
his nonverbal message clearly. However, the second driver
decoded the nonverbal message as a direction for him to

move to the bottom of the track. The result of this nonverbal miscommunication was a huge wreck. In corporate, business, or family life, nonverbal miscommunication can often have disastrous results.

Problem: Essentially, the problem with nonverbal communication is that few people even realize the messages they are sending nonverbally. Someone who is fidgeting during a job interview may be completely unaware of this nervous reaction. However, the interviewer, who is trying to select a PR spokesperson for the company, may bypass this candidate, based on nonverbal communication alone. I encourage leaders and potential leaders to take the time to study nonverbal communication and incorporate this knowledge into your organization. Used properly, nonverbal communication can be a positive and powerful dynamic in leadership training.

Summary

This chapter only scratches the surface regarding the significance of communication and the varieties and forms of communication available today. We didn't touch on electronic meetings, pagers, marketing materials, and a host of other communication options coming into vogue. Hopefully, you *have* seen how strong the brace of communications needs to be to support effective leadership. Without an effective communication process in place, the leader, those who select leaders, and those under leadership cannot be as productive as they should be. Communication, along with strategic planning, has to be an integral part of any organization if that organization is to realize success. Success cannot and will not just "happen." An organization doesn't improve by accident.

It needs careful attention and consistent maintenance to be the very best it can be for both internal and external customers.

Self-Assessment Exercise

1. The communication in our organization is:
   a. Excellent
   b. Good
   c. Average
   d. Below Average
   e. Poor

   If your answer is c, d, or e, why do you believe that to be the case?
   How will you address the problem?
   If your answer is a or b, why do you believe this to be the case?
   How can you verify your answer?

2. How do you know effective communication is taking place?

3. Do you spend adequate time training leaders and those under leadership in effective communication techniques?

4. Do you have a specific method to assess all forms of communication in your area of responsibility for effectiveness?

What will be your first act in evaluating and improving your personal communication techniques?

1   A. Long, "Administrative Shortage: Perception/Reality/Solutions," *IPLA Special Edition* 13 (May 2000): 3.

CHAPTER FIVE

BRACED ON PRINCIPLE: MORALS/ETHICS

Morals/Ethics

The last brace stabilizing the leadership tripod is *Morals and Ethics*. Please understand that I do not mean to impose my personal code of ethics on you, the reader. I simply want to underscore importance of the moral and ethical brace in sustaining a company's overall health and stability. Moral and ethical behavior should be modeled by leadership in all its forms–in leaders themselves, in those who select leaders, and in those under leadership.

However, it is not just enough to model these key traits. One leader's interpretation of what is ethical behavior may differ from another's in alarming ways. Consequently, leaders, those who select leaders, and those under leadership need a baseline from which to operate.

Establishing the Baseline

Certain character traits or core beliefs are common to most businesses, schools, or other organizations. Among these traits are honesty, respect, cooperation, and integrity. A company or organization needs to establish these core beliefs or values in order to gauge its purpose, progress, and success. These values should be the road map the company uses to make all its ethical and moral decisions.

Some examples of a company's set of values for ethical behavior might be:
- No gifts accepted over X dollars
- No alcohol at company functions
- No layoffs
- In advertising (no puffery)
- Timely payment of all vendors.

When everyone in an organization understands what is and is not acceptable company behavior, everyone also clearly understands the boundaries within which they are expected to operate. Understanding the boundaries means there is no room for individual interpretation of the company's ethical and moral standards.

What's the Bottom Line?

We've all heard stories about unethical business practices and corporations with the reputations for being "shark tanks." The media especially seems to revel in uncovering the latest corporate scandals. So, it's no surprise that much research has focused on the ethical practices of companies and organizations. What might surprise you, however, are the results of these studies. Over the long haul, companies that operate morally and ethically outperform those that don't. In looking at profit, the unethical firms may take a short-term lead, but that lead evaporates over time.

Let's look at the leadership tripod again, imagining that great boulder bearing down on the top piece. As we saw earlier, the tripod may stand for a while, but eventually it will collapse from the strain. Without braces, the legs will buckle. And it is my opinion that the most important brace of all is the Moral and Ethical brace. It must be the strongest brace.

But how do you know that this brace is as strong as it should be? How do you judge whether people in your business are operating morally and ethically, making moral and ethical decisions? Do you gauge this by the company's bottom line? By the company's retention rate? Attendance rate? Pay scale? Because your husband or wife says so?

My contention is that leaders, those who select leaders, or those under leadership need to have a concrete *method* by which to judge whether or not their companies and those working in those companies are operating according to the company's established core beliefs.

A Personal Model

I recognize that this is an area of personal choice and that you are entitled to set your own limits and boundaries. However, I would like to share a model that I use to judge whether decisions I make in my personal or professional life are ethical and moral. Each time I undergo this process, I take time to examine the values that undergird my professional and personal life.

To understand and explain the *Utility-Justice-Rights* model, I will use a real-life example from my family's recent business venture. We have decided to buy and renovate houses and then resell them or rent them. Of course, we automatically look for bargains! After laboring to fix them for resale or rental, we hope to make a profit. Not long ago a realtor called us and asked us to look at a house going up for absolute auction. Absolute auction means the house does not have to bring a base price; the highest bid, whatever it was, would buy the house. My son and I looked at the property, which was from an estate. To say it was a mess was an understatement. Our decision would be simple: were we going to buy it or not?

You might wonder how this could present a moral and ethical dilemma. The problem arose when we took ourselves through the *utility-justice-rights* process in order to come to a conclusion. Let us say for a moment that we decided to buy the property. Would that be an ethical and moral decision? Here is what we came up with by filtering our decision through the model. Note that there is no chronological order to the steps below. You may wish to arrange your model differently–just remember to examine all three points carefully.

Utility

Utilitarianism means, simply, do the benefits outweigh the costs? In this case we had to decide whether we would benefit financially by buying this house and reselling and/or renting it. We knew that we could probably rent the house to someone just the way it was. After all, people had been living in it, so people could live in it again. We could then justify the purchase of the home based solely on Utility.

This is the way many companies, leaders, and even those under leadership make decisions. Looking only to see if the benefits of a decision outweigh the costs, they go full speed ahead. This can have disastrous results. An example is a company that makes staffing decisions based on the doctrine of utility. Let's say the company lays off many of its employees. The short-term result, of course, is a ballooning of the bottom line. However, this short-term result will be eclipsed by the company's long-term failure to anticipate the real costs of the lay off–a loss of seasoned employees responsible for the efficient operation of the company's day-to-day business. This decision based on utility will come back to haunt them.

Justice

There are three kinds of justice–egalitarian, distributive, and retributive.

Egalitarian Justice

Egalitarian justice determines if you are treating all equally. In deciding whether to buy the house, we could with full confidence say this was not an issue. So, we were OK according to egalitarian justice.

In the organizational setting, leaders need to be certain they are treating those under their leadership in a fair and equal manner. For example, in deciding employee fringe benefits, it is not that the dollar amount has to be the same. Treating employees equally means treating those in similar job positions equitably. If a leader makes decisions "on a whim" or plays favorites, those decisions are not moral and ethical under the doctrine of egalitarianism.

Distributive Justice

Distributive justice asks the question, "Are you giving out what the others are giving in?" For us, this question would be phrased, "Are we going to charge rent on a reasonable basis for what the house is worth?" A second question would be phrased, "Are we going to get the house for what we think it is worth?" And still another, "Can we get out of it what we would have to put into it?"

Under the doctrine of distributive justice, we have some problems. First, we could probably get the house for a low

price, but would we get out of it what we would need to put
into it to bring it up to livable standards? The answer to this
would probably be no. Second, we could rent it just the way
it was, but whatever we charged would probably not measure
up to the doctrine of distributive justice. Those paying money
to live in the house would not be getting the value they
deserved for the money they paid.

In reality, at this point we stopped. Once we got ourselves
this far in the utility-justice-rights process, we could not go on
with the purchase. It would not be ethical and moral according to our core beliefs because the only way we could make
money would be to take rent on the property by leaving it the
way it was. Thus, the decision to buy the house would not be
just. However, for the sake of argument, let's follow the process to its farthest parameters.

Retributive Justice

Retributive justice is exemplified in this thought: people
get what they deserve based on their actions. Some would
justify renting a substandard house under this doctrine. They
might make a judgment that the family renting this house was
responsible for getting themselves into such a sorry situation,
so that in itself would justify taking their money and letting
them live in substandard conditions. While some other land-
lords might have been able to do this and satisfy their moral
and ethical standards, we wouldn't have been able to meet
our standards.

Even though we had already made our decision, let's pre-
tend that somehow we were able to get past the doctrine of
justice. There is still another measure of an ethical and moral
decision.

Rights

Two subsections fall under this category: positive rights and negative rights. These can be confusing to some, but they are important considerations in the process of deciding whether a decision is ethical and moral.

Positive rights are quality-of-life issues. If we were to purchase the house, we would ask ourselves, "Are we going to positively affect the quality of life of renters who might live in this house?" Of course, our answer would be another resounding NO! If somehow we could have justified the decision under utility and justice, we could never have classified this decision as ethical under the doctrine of positive rights. Putting someone in that house would most assuredly *not* improve his or her quality of life.

Negative rights are rights that cannot be taken from someone. These are the constitutional rights of life, liberty, and the pursuit of happiness. If somehow we had gotten this far in our decision to buy the house, we would fail again under the doctrine of negative rights. Putting someone in a slum-like house would not enhance his or her pursuit of happiness.

Summary: Counting the Cost

As you have probably already surmised, I consider the moral and ethical brace a critically important component of the leadership tripod. Without strong ethics and morals sustaining leadership at any level, success will be short lived. Longevity in leadership relies on a strong ethical and moral foundation. The individual standards, beliefs, and values may differ somewhat from company to company, but they need to be examined and assessed regularly, and they need to be effectively disseminated (communicated) throughout the organization.

Enron's collapse is a prime example of failure in the area of ethics and morals. In 2002 Enron had the sorry distinction of being the largest company ever to fail because of unethical accounting practices. The leaders of the organization were finally called to Washington to defend their behaviors. The ugly truth unearthed was that the leadership had operated in a totally utilitarian mind-set, allowing personal gain to outweigh the costs not only to those under their leadership but also to countless others outside the corporation. The whole flawed structure finally came down upon them, but not before many thousands of people had lost millions of dollars, their jobs, and their retirement funds. Had the leaders and decision-makers of Enron operated from an ethical and moral compass, the company might still be viable today.

Self-Assessment Exercise

1. Do you and/or your company have an established set of values and have those values been disseminated?

2. When weighing whether a decision is moral and ethical, do you filter that decision through a process like the *utility-justice-rights?*

CHAPTER SIX

IT'S FOUNDATIONAL CULTURE: BEHAVIOR AND BELIEFS

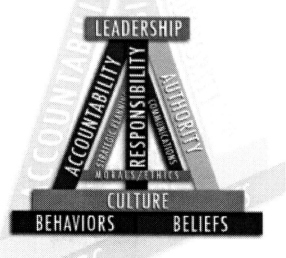

Behaviors and Beliefs

How do you ground leadership? The answer: By establishing and cultivating a solid base of *culture*. I would like the reader to examine the leadership tripod above and imagine the model without the firm base of culture beneath the legs. Even if the legs are structurally sound and the braces are strong, the tripod will function best on a level surface. A photographer working with a tripod in a mountainous region will often struggle to get his camera in place. By adjusting the tripod legs, he can manage to finally achieve enough balance to get the shot he wants. However, this often places undue stress on the tripod itself. If the photographer is not careful, the entire structure can topple, sending the camera crashing onto the rocks.

The same is true of leadership. Without a level, healthy culture beneath the tripod, leadership will perch precariously upon an unsound structure.

The Components of Culture

Many authors and scholars use the word *climate* interchangeably with *culture*. In defining "climate," *Webster's Dictionary* includes this description: *the prevailing influence or environmental conditions characterizing a group.* Regarding the word "culture," the dictionary says this: *the set of shared attitudes, values, goals, and practices that characterizes a company or corporation.* I think you can probably guess that I prefer the term *culture* because I think it much more clearly defines the attitudes, emotions, and general *feel* of the organization and its leadership. I also like what Webster's says elsewhere in its definition

of culture: *"the act of developing the intellectual and moral facul-
ties . . . expert care and training."*

Climate and culture consultants abound today. These
experts have written many articles and books, and regularly
conduct climate and culture audits for individuals, businesses,
and organizations. Their primary concern is to focus a company or individual on what to do to foster a healthy corporate environment. As we saw in chapter 3, many times these
consultants' very fine intentions result in a cumbersome,
expensive, and time-consuming process with little to show for
the effort. What is really needed is a simple model by which
a company can measure the health of its culture and learn to
cultivate the culture it really wants and needs.

A Lesson from the Bees

When explaining what comprises culture, I like to ask my
clients to imagine two bees buzzing around, and then I point
to a visual aid with a picture of bees. I tell them to think of
these bees as "cultured bees." And then, smiling, I explain that
culture is comprised of two "B's": *behaviors and beliefs.*

In the Tripod of Leadership model, the behaviors and
beliefs sit underneath the culture. Imagine what would happen if the behaviors and beliefs didn't match. All the components of a viable leadership structure would still be in place,
but the foundation would no longer be level. And that would
skew the structure enough to endanger it, causing leadership
to topple and the tripod to collapse. To have a healthy culture, a company and its leaders not only must have a system
of beliefs, but they also must behave in a way that matches
the beliefs they espouse.

Mixed Messages

Over the years as I have studied success and failure in leadership, I have found one constant that distinguishes those leaders and organizations that succeed from those that fail. Simply put, those who fail do not behave the way they *say* they believe. This inconsistency causes imbalance in the culture of the organization and sabotages effective leadership. *"Don't do as I do . . ."*

Families in chaos reflect this same inconsistency. In working with dysfunctional families, it seldom takes me long to find that the root cause of the problem is in the family's culture. The family's culture is unhealthy because they espouse one set of beliefs but then behave in a totally different manner.

Let's imagine a family in which Mom and Dad have told their children to be honest, to treat others fairly, and to honor commitments. We would call those good core beliefs, right?

Then the children observe Mom and Dad laughing because they did not report all of their income to the IRS. They hear Mom call in sick when she really just wants a day off. They hear Dad whispering on the phone, arranging to meet a woman for dinner. What do you think is going on in the minds of these children?

Because they see a mismatch of beliefs and behaviors, they do not have a healthy culture–a solid base–from which to operate. This causes confusion and mixed messages, all of which leads to why the family is dysfunctional and needs my help in figuring out why they are mixed up and messed up. Look around you. You probably won't have to look far to see a family in a similar situation.

"We value you, but . . ."

The same thing happens in the corporate world. Let's take a company that professes to value its employees, saying they are the most important part of the business. Then comes a sudden downturn in the economy. The company immediately lays off a third of its employees–but then gives raises to the corporate heads and/or stockholders. It's obvious the culture of the organization will be unhealthy because its behaviors don't match its beliefs. The employees will interpret the leadership's behavior as flagrant disregard for employee needs. That will, in turn, lead to indifference on their part: if the leadership doesn't care about us, why should we care about the organization?

Of course, there are times when a company cannot avoid a lay off. However, if a company is operating from a healthy culture, it will seriously and conscientiously consider all options before making the decision to disrupt employees' lives in this way. In the hypothetical case above, the leaders could have opted to forego their raises and instead redirected that money into the employees' payroll fund. The leaders' behaviors would then have matched their beliefs, proving to the employees that they did indeed value them as the most important part of the company.

Cultivating Culture

You might be wondering, "Is every failure due to an unhealthy culture?" The answer of course is NO. A business can fail for many reasons, just as a family can fall apart for many reasons. However, when analyzing the reason for failure–whether in family life or business–the first thing I examine is the behaviors and beliefs of all entities involved.

This works the same for successful businesses and families. If I were a betting man, I would bet you'd find a very healthy culture underlying that success. Beneath that healthy culture would be: 1) a sound belief structure that had been disseminated through the organization or family, and 2) a close match of the organizational/family behaviors to that belief system.

To expand on this, I would like to take some real-life examples of people we should all be familiar with from recent history.

It Depends on How You Define "Culture"

Former President Bill Clinton: When you look at the tripod model of leadership relative to the Clinton presidency, you can readily see that all the components of the tripod were in place–except the culture base, which was missing. Some would argue, instead, that his ethic and moral brace was damaged or missing. I disagree. He did have a set of ethics and morals, although they may not have been the same as yours or mine. The problem was with his culture. He espoused one set of beliefs to the American people and to the people of other countries, but he behaved in a much different manner. Thus, his credibility was undermined and he lost focus and effectiveness as a leader.

Jim Bakker: This successful television evangelist's story closely parallels Mr. Clinton's. But his charisma and success couldn't save him from disgrace. And it couldn't prevent the entire PTL organization from falling apart. The obvious "disconnect" of behaviors and beliefs eroded the culture and resulted in a major collapse.

Any dysfunctional family: You probably know one or at least have heard of one. Think about that family's patterns of behavior versus its beliefs. Are there incongruencies? You might also consider the latest pop culture family on "real" TV. Does this model work, or what?

A Balanced Life

There are plenty of examples to the contrary–stories of successful families, organizations, and leaders. Here are some of my favorites:

Billy Graham: If ever a man "walked the talk," it is this great man of God. For decades Billy Graham not only has made his beliefs evident, but has yet to exhibit any behavior that does not synchronize with his espoused beliefs. In everything I've heard and read about him, I have learned that his life is a portrait in consistency. Even though his crusades literally bring in millions of dollars, he has only taken a modest salary, making sure the rest goes back into his ministries. His behaviors match his beliefs!

Former Presidents Jimmy Carter and Harry Truman: While still in office, both of these presidents were maligned. Neither man was even expected to win the presidency. However, both, it seems to me, were men whose behaviors matched their beliefs. History is showing that both were effective leaders. I recently heard one historian characterize Jimmy Carter as the most intelligent president we have ever had. You see, in the short term, some may appear to be effective leaders. However, in the long term, those who live a balanced life–a life in which behaviors match beliefs–will stand the test of time.

George Huff: I have been blessed over the past thirty-five-plus years to be a part of the Huff family through marriage to my lovely wife, Carol. While I admire many in the Huff family, I am especially grateful to have known her father, the late George Huff. This family leader, whom I affectionately referred to as "Joe," always behaved in a manner that reflected what he believed. In all the years I knew Joe, I never saw anything in his behavior that contradicted his beliefs. His life was as amazingly consistent as Billy Graham's. He was giving, caring, and always put others before himself. Because he taught the same behaviors to his children, his legacy now lives on in our family and in the new families of our children. One man's balanced life has made a difference in countless lives.

Summary: A Firm Foundation

As we have seen, it takes more than a properly assembled tripod to ensure effective leadership. The tripod needs to rest on a firm base if it is to perform properly. That sound base is the culture, which is made up of the behaviors and beliefs of the leader, organization, or family unit. Keep that image of the tripod in your mind. It can have all the right components and be as strong as we can make it, but without a healthy culture to support it and keep it level, it could easily slip into the quicksand of failure.

Self-Assessment Exercise

1. Is the culture of your organization healthy? If not,
    why not? If so, what makes it healthy?

2. Is the culture of your family strong? If not, why not?
    If so, what makes it healthy?

3. As a leader, do your behaviors match your beliefs?
    a. 100% of the time
    b. 75% of the time
    c. 50% of the time

4. If you are not at the 100% level, how will you sys-
    tematically move yourself to the next level?

5. What organization or family can you share this
    knowledge with in the next thirty days?

SEVEN

INSIDE THE LEADER'S BRIEFCASE

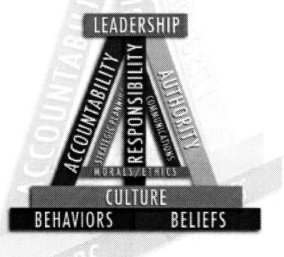

Inside the Leader's Briefcase

A tripod is not an end in itself. Its function is to support something. With that in mind, I've included a Leader's Briefcase alongside the model of the Leadership Tripod. In this briefcase are accessories that will both enhance leadership and improve the organization. The implements I am suggesting in this chapter are only a few of the many tools available to leadership. I hope you will feel free to add items as you see fit to enhance and improve your leadership. Of course, I hope you will share your information with me so that we can then share it with others who find the leadership tripod model useful.

The Telescope: Looking to the Future

Tripods and telescopes were meant for each other. On a starry night, or when some astronomical event is about to occur, we often see a telescope perched atop a tripod in someone's backyard. The telescope, of course, makes faraway things appear closer than they really are.

The first item the leader can and should have at the top of the Tripod of Leadership is a *telescope*. Leaders, those who select leaders, and those under leadership can benefit from the telescope's ability to see things at a distance and bring them closer. Every organization needs someone to be looking toward the future. Many times the future is closer than we really think, but we always need to think in future-oriented terms. A future-oriented perspective helps us plan ahead and keeps leadership on its competitive toes, poised and ready for change.

Just as the astronomer uses a telescope to look for threatening asteroids, the leader needs to be alert for those things that might harm the organization. Just as the astronomer uses a telescope to look for answers to science's many questions, the leader looks to the future for ways to strengthen and diversify the organization as a whole.

Putting Thought into It

Many planets are visible to the naked eye. But with a telescope, the astronomer can study planets with much more precision and see many more details. The same is true of the leader. Without taking the time to *THINK* about the future of leadership and the future of the organization, the leader and the organization operate without the full range of their capacities. The leader must carefully study what is "out there," just as the astronomer studies what is "out there." Otherwise, he or she limits the future to the here and now.

Visionary Thinking

The telescope of the leader is made up of two parts: *time* and *mind.* Leaders must take the time to think and must stretch their minds beyond their normal capacities.

The Ph.D. word for this kind of thinking is *metacognition;* i.e., thinking about thinking. Leaders must spend focused time using their minds as telescopes. This means looking to the future, troubleshooting options for growth, weighing possibilities, anticipating what needs to be accomplished today to prepare for tomorrow. This activity is a prime example of Theory SE Leadership. The leader must be out in front of the organization, looking to the future and leading the organization down the path of success.

In the last two organizations I led, I tried to impress the leaders with the importance of *visionary* (telescope) *thinking.* I not only encouraged this kind of thinking, but I also challenged them to take time each day to *"THINK."* I told them that if they were not *thinking* in at least an uninterrupted thirty-minute time block each day, they were not doing the job I needed them to do.

The Microscope: Up Close and Personal

The next item on this abbreviated list of implements for the Tripod of Leadership is a *microscope.* Of course, the microscope is used to make smaller things look larger. With the microscope we are able to see organisms in minute detail that are not normally visible to the naked eye. The scientist finds this tool to be indispensable not only for identifying specimens, but also for analyzing the small details, both positive and negative, that might have a huge impact on the organism.

Know Your Sheep

The same can be said for effective leaders. They must know the organization they are leading in precise detail. This does *not* mean micromanagement. The flaw in micromanagement is that it fails to keep the "big picture" in focus and threatens to weaken rather than strengthen the organization. It focuses on the negatives and the "we can'ts."

Using a microscope approach means the leader has an intrinsic understanding of how the organization operates at all levels. This leader focuses on the positives and the "we cans," looking for mutually beneficial ways to edify and strengthen the organization. We could call this Theory SE Leadership and we could sum up its philosophy this way: "Know your sheep; know your flock."

The microscope is especially helpful when the leadership is creating the brace of strategic planning. It helps in evaluating an organization's competition, assessing the opportunities for cooperation, identifying organizational flaws, and highlighting organizational strengths. Careful analysis of the organization can help the leader, those who select leaders, and those under leadership to decide on ways to fix the problems they see under the microscope. Peering through this instrument also gives numerous opportunities to celebrate the organization's successes.

The Camera: A Picture's Worth

The Leader's Briefcase contains the *telescope* to help leaders prepare for the future. It also contains the *microscope* to help leaders manage the details. What can help leaders attain continuity in organizational planning? In other words, what can help them relate or connect an organization's present state to its past?

Pointed at the Present

When first contemplating the *camera* on the Leadership Tripod, I thought of the snapshot as it captures a moment in the present. Of course, this is important for the leader, those who select leaders, and those under leadership. This camera really captures the *mission* of the organization in the Strategic Plan Brace. What is the organization about today? How am I leading today? These are questions the camera can and should answer.

In the strategic planning process, this analysis helps the organization and the leaders drive stakes in the road to continuous improvement. As a leader you must have a handle on where you are today before you can plan where you are going tomorrow. *Otherwise, if you don't know where you are, how will you know where to go or even when you get there?* Leaders need to take snapshots of the organization and all its components to be sure they know where they are *now*.

A Look Back

The camera's uses obviously are not limited to the present. We must also remember the pictures we have taken in the past, the history of the organization and its leadership. When families get together for reunions, they often dig out the photograph albums. Looking at old pictures can jog our memories–helping us recall how things used to be, how far we've come, how much we've changed.

The same is true in the organizational setting. Old pictures can help us remember how the organization has changed, what decisions prompted those changes, what decisions should have had more forethought. Effective leaders need to build on those snapshots, stressing their importance and urging the organization not to forget its history.

Of course, this historical perspective (the old snapshots) should not paralyze the organization and its leadership in a time warp of regret, so that it longs for things "to be like they used to be." That would be paramount to looking at old high school pictures and wishing we were as young and slim as we were then. *If we sit and ponder too long what once was, we will never experience what might be.* Conversely, if we don't use our history to help us make informed decisions, we will be in danger of making catastrophic mistakes.

Photographing the Flock

The Theory S leader would use the camera to take snapshots of his flock as a group, as they are in that moment of time. He would also photograph each sheep in the flock, taking note of any new lambs. He or she could then pull out pictures taken earlier and compare the old photos to the new ones. The new photos would clearly show how lambs had grown and matured. The old photos might also reveal a lamb or sheep missing from the new group photograph. This could be a valuable lesson in helping to determine why that sheep was no longer with the flock. If the sheep was lost because of a mistake, steps could then be taken to prevent such a mistake from occurring in the future.

The Transit: Establishing Boundaries

Of the instruments I have chosen to place on top of the Tripod of Leadership, this is one most people will seldom come across in their daily activities. Just because the *transit* is not found in the average toolbox does not diminish its importance. You see them occasionally at construction sites or in areas that are being developed. One person will be peering through an instrument on a tripod. Some distance away, another person will be holding a stick with markings. They are using the transit to survey the land and establish boundaries.

Why does the effective leader or organization need to use a transit? Since you've come this far in the book, the answer should now be apparent. An organization, leader, those who select leaders, and those under leadership need to know the boundaries within which they will operate. When engineers finish their work with the transit, they submit a detailed report of their findings. The leader must do the same, making everyone aware of the organization's boundaries, the individual tasks to be completed within those boundaries, and the plan for the continuous improvement of the organization and everyone in it.

When positioned on the tripod, this instrument assists the leader in the *Responsibility* leg of leadership, as well as in *Authority* and *Accountability.* It also, in a macro sense, is used to complete the brace of *Strategic Planning.*

The Shepherd's Transit

The Theory S (SE) leader would consider his transit to be a shepherd's staff. The "tool kit" of the eastern shepherd always includes a staff, which is used both as an offensive and defensive weapon. Comparing the transit to a staff in this case would be to highlight its use as an offensive tool: to keep the sheep in the flock. The shepherd sets boundaries on how far to let one of the flock stray. When a sheep wanders past those boundaries, the shepherd hooks the curved portion of the staff around the animal and gently pulls it back into the fold. Just as the shepherd needs to set boundaries and the sheep need to be aware of them, the leader, those who select leaders, and those under leadership also must be aware of their boundaries. It's not a matter of "limiting" an organization or team member's potential. It's a matter of setting parameters and then framing them.

Summary: Tools that Enhance

In this chapter I have highlighted only a few of the many tools or instruments that could be used effectively on the Leadership Tripod. My hope, however, is that you will see how the model can spur thinking, encouraging all the stakeholders in an organization to think differently and using the model as a springboard for continuous improvement.

But always think in positive terms. For example, someone might decide to set a *laser* atop the tripod. True, a laser could be an efficient tool to pinpoint problems and slice out areas of unproductivity. It could also be used to micromanage or split apart the organization. Any additional tools a leader, those who select leaders, or those under leadership want to add to the briefcase must be carefully examined to ensure they strengthen and not weaken the Leadership Tripod.

Self-Assessment Exercise

1. Are you a visionary thinker? What evidence would you give to support your answer?

2. How aware are you of the details of the organization you lead? What evidence would you give to support your answer?

3. If someone asked the question, "Where is your organization today?" how would you answer the question and what evidence would you give to support your answer?

4. How do the stakeholders you lead know what the organization's boundaries are and/or their specific positions within those boundaries?

5. What additional tools could you add to the leader's briefcase and how do you think they would strengthen the model?

CONCLUSION

PALETTE OF KNOWLEDGE

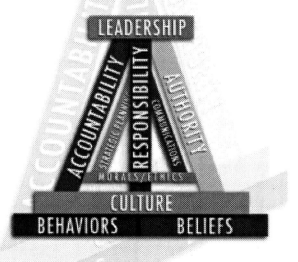

Palette of Knowledge

In this author's humble opinion, leadership is an **ART**. It is something one must continue to perfect, practice, and perform. Although some leaders may have more inborn skills and abilities to lead than others, that does not mean they are equipped for life. All leaders, whether novices or those with years under their belts, need to continually build on their skill and knowledge base in order to continue experiencing success in leadership.

You might have already realized that in the previous chapter I left out one very recognizable use for the tripod–to support an artist's canvas. We call such a tripod an easel. The artist places a canvas on the easel to free his or her hands to hold the palette and paintbrush. The palette holds the individual colors into which the artist will dip the paintbrush, skillfully transferring those colors to the canvas. In the right combination and under the artist's watchful eye, paint and canvas will meet in a creative display of art.

I would like to finish my discussion of the Tripod of Leadership with that picture in the reader's mind. Instead of thinking of a palette of colors, I would like the reader to think of this book as a Palette of Knowledge. The effective leader must take the colors of knowledge discussed in this book and paint them onto the canvas of leadership. When skillfully applied in the right proportions, these colors create a beautiful and worthwhile portrait of the effective leader.

The Right Mix

On this Palette of Knowledge are, of course, all the different *leadership theories.* If leaders are to create an accurate portrait of leadership, they must have all the colors (theories) of leadership at their disposal. Using only one theory would be like expecting the painter to use one color to create a portrait of someone. This portrait might resemble the person, but it would be one-dimensional, limiting the extent to which the artist could capture the individual's true likeness.

Likewise, if the painter used only primary colors and did not mix one with the other, the painting would be garish and unrealistic. By mixing colors, just as in mixing theories, the painter can capture the subtle nuances and idiosyncrasies that make each person unique. Using all the knowledge available to them, leaders can create leadership portraits that are distinctive, versatile, and applicable to a variety of situations.

The Right Support

This Palette of Knowledge works in conjunction with the easel, which is supported by the legs of *Authority, Accountability,* and *Responsibility.* All three legs must work together to hold the canvas at the proper angle. If the easel is off balance, the canvas may tumble to the ground, ruining the painting.

The braces of *Strategic Planning, Communication,* and *Ethics and Morals* contribute to the strength of the easel, ensuring the portrait can fulfill its destiny as a masterpiece.

The Right Foundation

If the artist is worrying that the easel might slip at any moment, he or she will not be focused on the primary task of painting. As well, the artist may have to put down the palette and even the paintbrush occasionally in order to make adjustments to the easel. This causes an interruption in the flow of creative ideas. We have learned from our study that the leadership tripod has to sit on a firm foundation if it is to function properly. This foundation or base is the *culture* of the organization, reinforced by the organization's *beliefs* and *behaviors*.

So, too, with the artist's tripod or easel. If the easel rests securely on a sound base, the artist will have more freedom to exercise the creative aspects of his or her craft. If the artist isn't worrying about whether the easel will hold the canvas, he or she will not be distracted and can instead tend to the many details of the painting. This includes tending to the craft of painting itself. An artist may have a picture in mind of what the completed painting will look like. To achieve that, he or she will not scoop up paint indiscriminately and start hurling it at the canvas. That would clearly demonstrate a disparity between beliefs and behaviors. The true artist follows a method, painstakingly working to apply the picture in his or her mind to the canvas. The true artist also hopes that each new painting will show improvement over the last.

The Right Tools

In addition to the easel, canvas, and palette, the artist needs special paintbrushes to create a portrait. These brushes are the tools in the *Briefcase of Leadership*. Just as the artist needs brushes of different sizes and types, the leader needs the Telescope, Microscope, Camera, and Transit. Each brush the artist uses has a specific purpose. Some create lines. Some are used to slather on great amounts of paint. Some are used to apply delicate pinpricks of color. All contribute to making the individual elements of the portrait come together into a single work of art.

The same is true with the tools in the briefcase. Each is used for a different purpose, but all are needed to ensure that the portrait of leadership is as complete and accurate as it can be.

My hope and prayer for you as a leader is that your canvas will portray the most accurate picture of leadership possible. An artist without a full Palette of Knowledge cannot complete the portrait. If you do not continue to add to your Palette, refilling and refreshing each color and adding new colors, your portrait will not attain its full potential. And that is what leadership is all about—being all you can be and helping others to do the same.

Appendix

Sample Corporation
Strategic Plan
2002-2003

Vision

Sample Corporation will be a leader in construction quality and service to all clients. All those who deal with and are affected by Sample Corporation will know it as a company of honesty and integrity.

Mission

Sample Corporation partners with clients, subcontractors, and fellow employees in providing quality projects while establishing positive relationships and maintaining the highest level of integrity. As a team, Sample builds on experience leading to being more creative and efficient in meeting present and future needs of the community.

Goals/Objectives

We believe we are and need to continue to be financially stable.

1. We will examine and make appropriate changes in our bidding and cost estimating, as well as becoming more selective in our project selection process, by September 1, 2002.
2. We will establish target markets by June 1, 2002.
3. We will establish and implement a financial incentive program for all staff by April 1, 2003.

We believe we are and should continue to be a company of integrity and honesty.

1. We will revise the customer satisfaction survey to include feedback on integrity and honesty by August 2002 and fully implement the survey by October1, 2002.
2. We will prepare and disseminate job descriptions for all staff.
3. We will develop an assessment process and review process for all staff by April 15, 2003. A part of this process will focus on integrity and honesty.

We believe in completing quality construction projects.

1. We will strive to have 100% of all contracts signed and delivered for all jobs before they begin by September 1, 2002.
2. We will compile subcontractor lists and differentiate them in categories by July 1, 2002.
3. We will formalize a system of assessment of subcontractors for site superintendents by June 1, 2002.

We believe marketing is a team effort.

1. We will establish target markets by June 1, 2002.
2. We will determine current market share by June 1, 2002.
3. We will obtain ten (10) new clients by April 1, 2002.

4. We will develop market ancillaries and distribute to all staff by June 1, 2002.

5. We will implement our Web site by September 1, 2002.

We believe in effective communication.

1. We will begin a weekly communication from Steve via E-mail by April 15, 2002.

2. We will establish monthly superintendent meetings by April 30, 2002.

3. We will conduct quarterly meetings with all staff.

4. We will conduct at least two social activities by April 1, 2003.

Personal Vision, Mission Statements
Personal/Professional Goals
January 2002

Vision Statement:
I will leave this world with a legacy for those who follow and, above all things, be remembered as a "man of God."

Mission Statement:
In all things I do, I will attempt to approach each person or activity as a man of God. I will attempt to be a man of integrity and treat all those I deal with in a respectful manner. I will at all times attempt to be a solid Christian, a good husband, father, grandfather, friend, employee, and person.

Personal Goals and Objectives:

1. Be a better Christian.
   a. I will read a minimum of one chapter of the Bible per day.
   b. I will get more involved in church activities.
   c. I will continue to pray daily.
   d. I will continue my work with J. R. to try and get his time reduced.
   e. I will faithfully complete my duties as a member of the leadership council.
   f. I will finish my training for being a lay counselor.

2. Be a better Husband.
   a. I will do something special for my wife on a minimum of a weekly basis.

b. I will think of my wife's needs first.

c. I will help around the house without being asked.

d. I will go to camp with her if she is assigned.

3. Be a better Father.
   a. I will be aware of my children's needs and help to meet them.
   b. I will be available more for all my kids.
   c. I will do something "special" with each or all.
   d. I will be more positive and affirming in my relationships with my children.

4. Be a better Grandfather.
   a. I will spend quality time with each of my grandchildren.
   b. I will allow and celebrate their individual differences.
   c. I will attend their activities.

5. Be a better Friend.
   a. I will call my friends and/or write them notes of encouragement.
   b. I will keep a log of my contacts with my friends.
   c. I will cultivate and deepen relationships in our small group.

6. Be a better Person.
   a. I will take better care of myself by losing weight.
   b. I will exercise a minimum of three times per week for 30 minutes.
   c. I will read recreationally at least six books through 2002 and log those books.

    d. I will increase my personal savings account by year's end.

    e. I will spend less time watching TV and more time in developing relationships.

Professional Goals/Objectives:

1. Be a better Employee
    a. I will increase my expectations for all my students and grade them accordingly.
    b. I will attempt to find ways to help at the university to improve their teacher education programs.
    c. I will complete all consulting duties in a timely fashion.

POST-ASSESSMENT TEST

Note to the reader: Please take this test after you have read the book.

1. In your organization, what is the level of knowledge in leadership theory and application for each of the following groups?

   Those selecting leaders:

5	4	3	2	1
High	Moderate	Neutral	Some	None

   The leaders themselves:

5	4	3	2	1
High	Moderate	Neutral	Some	None

   Those under leadership:

5	4	3	2	1
High	Moderate	Neutral	Some	None

2. Are each group's job and/or leadership responsibilities clearly stated?

   Those selecting leaders:

5	4	3	2	1
High	Moderate	Neutral	Some	None

The leaders themselves:

5	4	3	2	1
High	Moderate	Neutral	Some	None

Those under leadership:

5	4	3	2	1
High	Moderate	Neutral	Some	None

3. Does each group have authority to clearly carry out its responsibilities?

Those selecting leaders:

5	4	3	2	1
High	Moderate	Neutral	Some	None

The leaders themselves:

5	4	3	2	1
High	Moderate	Neutral	Some	None

Those under leadership:

5	4	3	2	1
High	Moderate	Neutral	Some	None

4. Are accountability systems clearly established for each group?

Those selecting leaders:

5	4	3	2	1
High	Moderate	Neutral	Some	None

The leaders themselves:

5	4	3	2	1
High	Moderate	Neutral	Some	None

Those under leadership:

5	4	3	2	1
High	Moderate	Neutral	Some	None

5. Is there a strategic plan in place for each group and is it clearly understood and used as a base of reference for all decisions?

Those selecting leaders:

5	4	3	2	1
High	Moderate	Neutral	Some	None

The leaders themselves:

5	4	3	2	1
High	Moderate	Neutral	Some	None

Those under leadership:

5	4	3	2	1
High	Moderate	Neutral	Some	None

6. How would you rate the communication lines within each group (intra-communication)?

   Those selecting leaders:

5	4	3	2	1
High	Moderate	Neutral	Some	None

   The leaders themselves:

5	4	3	2	1
High	Moderate	Neutral	Some	None

   Those under leadership:

5	4	3	2	1
High	Moderate	Neutral	Some	None

7. How would you rate the communication lines between each group (inter-communication)?

   Those selecting leaders:

5	4	3	2	1
High	Moderate	Neutral	Some	None

   The leaders themselves:

5	4	3	2	1
High	Moderate	Neutral	Some	None

Those under leadership:

5	4	3	2	1
High	Moderate	Neutral	Some	None

8. Are the organization's ethics and morals clearly stated and evident?

Those selecting leaders:

5	4	3	2	1
High	Moderate	Neutral	Some	None

The leaders themselves

5	4	3	2	1
High	Moderate	Neutral	Some	None

Those under leadership:

5	4	3	2	1
High	Moderate	Neutral	Some	None

9. Is the culture (climate) of the organization healthy and do the behaviors and beliefs of each group match that culture?

Those selecting leaders:

5	4	3	2	1
High	Moderate	Neutral	Some	None

The leaders themselves:

5	4	3	2	1
High	Moderate	Neutral	Some	None

Those under leadership:

5	4	3	2	1
High	Moderate	Neutral	Some	None

10. How important do you think the concept of leadership is to each of the groups below?
    Those selecting leaders:

5	4	3	2	1
High	Moderate	Neutral	Some	None

The leaders themselves:

5	4	3	2	1
High	Moderate	Neutral	Some	None

Those under leadership:

5	4	3	2	1
High	Moderate	Neutral	Some	None

11. What have you gained from reading Leadership Tripod? How will you put this knowledge into practice in your workplace, family, or any organization with which you are affiliated?